Pay Attention!

Pay Attention!

HOW TO **Listen, Respond,** AND **Profit** FROM **Customer Feedback**

ANN THOMAS • JILL APPLEGATE

WILEY

John Wiley & Sons, Inc.

Contents

Acknowledgments

Writing a book on a topic like the new voice of the customer and social media is a bit like trying to hit a moving target. Before it's even published, there will be new sites, applications, and research that will perhaps offer new insights. Nonetheless, we opted to tackle it. Recognizing how intimately connected these new communication channels are to service made it an energizing and educational experience for us, but one we embraced with zeal and enthusiasm.

Because we continue to hear story after story from family, friends, clients, and workshop participants, we realize that focusing on delivering and differentiating based on service continues to be a challenge for organizations everywhere. A thank-you goes out to all those willing to share their stories and experiences, good and bad. And thank you to those who, knowing we were writing this book, provided links to articles, blogs, and research that supported our effort. As challenging and big as this topic is, we realize it is a lot of ground to cover.

A huge thanks goes to editor extraordinaire, Dave Zelinski. Dave kept us motivated, inspired, and on task and provided invaluable insight. Without question, this endeavor would have been nearly impossible without him; he's one in a million and we would not want to do one of these books without him.

A very special thank-you to Susan Zemke, whose enthusiasm and excitement for this book and all that we do is so appreciated. We are grateful to Susan for her constant support and commitment to Performance Research Associates.

We're delighted to be part of the John Wiley & Sons family. We've thoroughly enjoyed partnering with their team. Thank you to editor Dan Ambrosio for his support and belief in the project.

Ann wishes to thank all those who listened, cajoled, and offered insights. Through their love and support, her family—Jim, Maggie, Shana, and Kate—always plays a big role in getting through an overwhelming project. The "hun" proved a wonderful resource for his insights about new technology and marketing. Thanks Attila. And to those clients and friends who responded quickly and thoughtfully—too many to list—you helped make this book the best by sharing your real-time experiences.

Jill would like to thank her family and friends for their love and constant support throughout this process; they were with her, encouraging her to look toward the finish line, all the way.

None of this would have been possible without the groundbreaking work started by Ron Zemke in 1985. Ron's efforts in the world of service quality are near legendary. We are honored to have a small part in continuing his efforts.

Introduction

Those tasked with serving today's customers face a challenge unlike almost any encountered by their predecessors. Identifying and meeting customer needs has always been a tricky task, given shifting expectations, ever-changing market realities, and the desire by many for the full "value" package: low prices, great product quality, and top-notch service.

But today's consumers are a different breed. They are, by and large, a more skeptical, demanding, and self-reliant bunch, and they have more ways than ever to speak back to companies about the quality of their product or service offerings. All of this makes the customer service challenge more difficult, yet more important, than ever before.

Today's customers are more wary of corporate marketing messages and more likely to seek out and rely on the experiences of peers, or "people like me," before making their buying decisions. They're prone to research those purchases with the fervor of investigative journalists, trusting their own data more than the lofty marketing claims of businesses that too often have let them down in the past, or retail "experts" looking to score a big commission. It's a skepticism born in the Enron age and hardened during the recent economic collapse, when many once-trusted companies and business icons folded or had ethical lapses.

Today's customer also speaks with a more omnipresent voice via blogs, social networks and the discussion boards, or public and corporate web sites, where they frequently weigh in with rants, recommendations and lessons learned about their interactions with businesses. No longer can companies expect to receive feedback only through 800 numbers, e-mail messages, or hard-copy surveys and in private.

It's on these Web-based channels that a growing segment of your customer base feels most comfortable sharing opinions and swapping experiences. It's also here where companies have an unprecedented opportunity to listen in and get a candid "warts and all" look at how they're perceived in the marketplace, as well as to offer advice and service assistance that can spread goodwill and create passionate advocates for their brands.

Every day corporate reputations are enhanced or besmirched by commentary in the blogosphere and social media. When customers are upset or disappointed by their dealings with companies, these new online channels offer a powerful way for them to strike back at the perceived offenders. Examples of rude, disrespectful, or indifferent customer service are likely to be replayed and retold across cyberspace or show up as mocking videos on YouTube that receive millions of hits.

These fundamental changes make the Pay Attention strategy we detail in this book, one grounded in years of service quality research, important to maintaining a competitive edge. It's a philosophy based, first and foremost, in the knowledge that delivering consistently high levels of service quality can be a profit driver. More than 12 years of research from the renowned American Customer Satisfaction Index (ACSI), run by the University of Michigan's School of Business, has shown that customer satisfaction is a leading indicator of company financial performance. Simply put, stocks of companies with high ACSI scores tend to do better than those of companies with low scores.

The Pay Attention strategy begins with crawling inside the minds of your customers to understand what keeps them loyal—or prone to defection—and to get an unfiltered look at how they perceive your product or service offerings versus the competition. That requires not only traveling to new online channels where customers make their voices heard but viewing what's said there as a gift and not a nuisance, understanding that until customer preferences or pet peeves are exposed to the light of day, there is little you can do to fix what's perceived as wrong and keep doing what's right. It's about incorporating the new voice of the customer into all aspects of your operations.

Paying Attention also means being fanatical about the fundamentals that make customer service a competitive distinguisher. The care that you take in hiring, training, compensating, and rewarding those who do the often thankless job of serving customers, whether in call centers, on sales floors, or in checkout lanes, is essential to creating a service edge. These are the people whose performance in countless Moments of Truth on the front lines either makes or breaks your service reputation and your ability to keep valuable customers in the fold.

It's also about paying close attention to the customer experience, ensuring that your systems, policies, and practices make you ETDBW—easy to do business with—rather than frustrate, confuse, or upset customers who increasingly have little time in their lives for additional headache or hassle.

Finally, paying attention means capitalizing on new and emerging technologies to listen to and serve your customer base. Not every organization faces the same urgency to engage their customers on social media, since consumers in some industries don't yet rely on tools such as Facebook or Twitter as much as others. But it's important to get started, because although specific services may come and go, online networks that enable customers to connect around similar interests or buying needs are here to stay. Ditto for the blog technology that gives customers a powerful new megaphone and means of influencing corporate reputations.

At its core the Pay Attention strategy is deceptively simple: It's about making the meeting of a basic human need—the one for customers to feel heard, dealt with fairly, and treated like someone of import—a core component of business strategy, one emphasized by management and executed by customer care staff on a daily basis.

Take that concept to heart and you'll not only feel better about yourself and your organization, you'll also see ample benefits accrue to your bottom line.

Pay Attention!

Chapter 1

PAY ATTENTION TO TODAY'S CUSTOMERS

When two rogue employees at Domino's Pizza decided to have some fun with a video camera, they had no idea they were about to provide the business world with a powerful lesson in the new voice of the customer.

The employees filmed a prank video of themselves stuffing cheese up their noses and then putting it on Domino's sandwiches. As one of the employees appears to tamper with the food, the other is heard saying: "In about five minutes this will be sent out on delivery where someone will actually be eating it." The two then posted the video to YouTube, the popular video-sharing site, where it proceeded to get more than a million hits over a few days.

News of the video spread like wildfire on social media sites such as Twitter and Facebook, and it wasn't until a sympathetic blogger alerted Domino's to the offensive posting that it was finally removed.

Domino's response was textbook. Its president posted his own YouTube video apologizing for the incident and repeatedly stressing that it was a misguided joke. "There is nothing more important or sacred to us than our customers' trust," said CEO Patrick Doyle. "It sickens me that the act of two individuals could impact our great system." But the damage to the brand was already done. According to the research firm YouGov, which surveys some 1,000 consumers every day, the perception of Domino's quality went from positive to negative in just a few days. Untold numbers of loyal Domino's customers were likely second guessing their relationship, wondering if they could trust the pizza maker to deliver untampered food in the future.

Further evidence of the new ways that customers are speaking to companies—and how some of the most service-savvy organizations are speaking back—came in an incident involving Comcast Corp., the cable provider. When a prominent blogger, Michael Arrington, complained on his site about a frustrating outage with his Comcast cable service, no one was more shocked than the blogger when a Comcast executive responded *within 20 minutes* to his complaint, making sure a technician was quickly sent out to fix the problem.

The blogger reported that he first notified the company of the problem by phone, but service staff there had no clue as to when the problem could be fixed. The Comcast executive's swift response was part of a new program called Comcast Cares, created to actively monitor Twitter and other social media sites and respond to customer comments about the company. The program is designed to buttress, not replace, e-mail and phone help channels and respond to pressing customer concerns with greater speed.

Rather than forcing customers to call an 800 number and endure a wait on hold or send e-mail that isn't answered for 24 hours, Comcast service reps can simply "tweet" customers to quickly acknowledge problems and set the recovery process in motion—engaging customers in a communication channel in which many are increasingly comfortable.

The Power of Online Megaphones

Long gone are the days when customers made their voices heard only through 800 numbers, e-mail messages, or face-to-face interactions or by telling neighbors over the back fence how horrible—or surprisingly wonderful—was the service they received at the dry cleaner, local restaurant, bank, or web site. Now they more commonly speak through the virtual megaphones known as Twitter, Facebook, MySpace, and other social networking sites as well as by posting reviews of businesses they frequent on sites like Yelp or CitySearch. Many more make their voices heard through discussion boards and dedicated product review areas on company web sites. Although accurate user numbers are hard to come by, it's safe to say many millions of people are using these tools on a daily basis.

"An entire generation is growing up that will never dial a 1-800 number to reach customer care," says Amanda Mooney, a digital media strategist with Edelman Digital, a division of Edelman Public Relations.

But it isn't just teenagers or 20-somethings using social media. According to a 2009 study from Pew Internet and the American Life Project, the median age of Facebook users is now 33, up from 26 in May 2008; the median age of Twitter users is 31 and LinkedIn users is 39. Businesses of all sizes also have become regular users of social networks to market products, keep tabs on consumer opinions, and engage customers on the turf where they feel most comfortable.

When today's customers are upset by customer service experiences, the first place many turn to vent their frustrations is the Web. A 2008 study by TARP Worldwide Inc., an Arlington, Virginia-based customer service research firm, found, for example, that 12 percent of dissatisfied online customers told their "buddy lists" about the experience—lists that average more than 60 persons. On average, four times more people on the Web hear about negative experiences than positive ones, according to TARP research.

Consider the experience of professional guitarist Dave Carroll. Carroll was unable, after a full year of negotiation, to receive any compensation from United Airlines for having his guitar damaged by baggage handlers—damage requiring $1,200 in repairs. Carroll had been at O'Hare Airport in Chicago, en route between Halifax, Canada, and Nebraska, when a passenger next to him noticed that baggage handlers were throwing guitar cases on the tarmac outside the plane.

Frustrated by the airline's response, Carroll decided to write and post a song titled "United Breaks Guitars" to YouTube. The song proved an instant sensation that received more than 600,000 hits within a week, and as of this printing, has received more than 7 million hits. According to news reports, United representatives called Carroll after the video went viral and said they wanted to discuss the situation. To the airline's credit, it was considering using the reputation-damaging video as a case study for how to better handle future customer complaints.

Although it's impossible to control everything customers say about your company on social networks or in the blogosphere, shrewd companies have figured out that there are effective ways to manage their reputations online. One such tactic is to try to redirect negative commentary, getting customers to talk directly to your company rather than to broadcast their displeasure to millions of Web users. The idea is to try to harness the conversation and thus control more of it.

Such interventions increase the odds of positive outcomes and mitigate the potential damage caused by letting rumors or "viral sharing" of bad service experiences go unchecked for long periods on the Internet. Dell Computer, for example, is among the growing number of organizations using sophisticated tracking software to monitor comments made about the company on social networks and the blogosphere, often joining these conversations to try to solve problems or answer questions. Although customers may initially have viewed this behavior as intrusive, many have grown to embrace the service assistance, with the caveat that it's handled deftly.

Negative service experiences spread like wildfire, even without the aid of technology. When we feel disrespected, talked down to, treated like a number, or just plain poorly served by an organization, we're eager to share that experience with friends, work colleagues, relatives, and anyone who will lend an ear. The sharing carries a warning: Steer clear of the offending company. Consider the multiplying factor, then, when people write about those "service experiences from hell" on their blogs, user groups, or social networking pages. Untold numbers around the globe are likely to read them, especially if they are particularly well told or the company in question has done something that offends a sense of fairness.

A More Skeptical and Distrustful Customer

Whether wholly true or not, tales of service woe or service excellence have an impact on those who read them, especially if those people have no prior experience with the organization. And that perception, when acted on, can mean the difference between sales realized and sales lost.

That's because today's customers are much more likely to believe in and trust the experiences of their peers or other consumers than they are corporate marketing messages. According to a 2008 study by the Society for New Communications Research (SNCR), 74 percent of active Internet users choose companies or brands based on the experiences of others that they read about online. Additional research, conducted in 2007 by Edelman Public Relations as part of its annual "trust barometer" study, found that people's most credible source of information was "a person like me," which for the first time surpassed even academic experts and doctors on the trust scale.

Commented Richard Edelman, head of the public relations firm, about the study findings: "We have reached an important juncture, where the lack of trust in established institutions and figures of authority has motivated people to trust their peers as the best sources of information about a company. Companies need to move away from sole reliance on top-down messages delivered to elites toward fostering peer-to-peer dialogue among consumers, activating a company's most credible advocates."

Today's customers also are more prone to conduct exhaustive research about products or services before making buying decisions, a process made easier by the volume of comparative data available on the Internet regarding prices, features, reliability, performance, and more. According to the SNCR study, 72 percent of respondents research companies' customer care history online prior to purchasing products and services.

What Does This All Mean for Your Own Customer Service Strategy?

For starters, if you're not giving customers an online outlet for expressing their opinions about your products, services, or overall operations, you're likely raising suspicion or even being left behind your competitors. Research shows that consumers are increasingly skeptical of companies that don't encourage reviews of their offerings on a corporate web site. Many believe it means you have something you're trying to hide.

Organizations that don't solicit comments, reviews, or ratings are often afraid they'll get too many negative ones, but the reality is that some less than glowing comments mixed in with pats on the back add credibility to the site. We've all read review sites that feature nothing but positive commentary that reads as though it's written by the CEO's mother or a book author's husband. Shrewd companies such as Amazon.com have begun displaying their most useful positive reviews side by side with their most useful negative reviews, a process many customers find helpful in making buying decisions. Other companies are regularly sending customers e-mails that feature online ratings or reviews, and many find that products with customer reviews have a significantly lower return rate than those without them.

Most service-savvy organizations also realize that there are nuggets of gold to be mined in this new, albeit more skeptical, voice of the customer. By tapping into what customers are saying about them in unfiltered settings such as social networks or blogs, companies can gather information and insight that can help tweak service performance, capture ideas for product enhancements, improve marketing campaigns, or upgrade their web sites based on user suggestions.

The best of these companies also view their front-line customer service staff—those working in call centers, standing behind counters, strolling sales floors, or on teams dedicated to crawling social media sites—as the canaries in the coal mine of customer service. Well before anyone else in the organization, they usually know about emerging problems with service quality, recurring issues, or breakdowns that are driving customers into the embrace of the competition. They interact with customers each and every day and thus have intimate knowledge of where the company is meeting their needs and where it is falling short.

In that sense they are essential "listening posts" of the organization and a key piece in tracking the new voice of the customer. Organizations that are truly interested in customers' unvarnished opinions of their service quality regularly make a point of surveying their frontline staff to help identify, and shore up, weak spots in their service delivery systems.

Rising Global Service Expectations

If you're part of an organization dedicated to listening to the new voice of the customer, you'll know that expectations for service quality are rising and have been doing so for a number of years.

According to the *2008 Customer Satisfaction Survey* conducted by Accenture, the global management consulting firm—a survey that queried 4,189 people in eight countries across five continents—52 percent of respondents said that their expectations for customer service were higher than in the period five years before. The trend toward rising expectations was found in both mature and emerging markets; in fact, the survey found that "expectations of consumers in emerging markets are rising at an alarming rate." To wit: 84 percent of survey respondents in China, India, and Brazil said that their expectations for quality service were higher than they were five years ago.

The Accenture survey also found—for the fourth consecutive year—that the number of consumers who left a company because of poor service was significantly higher than the number who left because they *found a lower price elsewhere*. In addition, only 45 percent of respondents reported that their service expectations were frequently or always met.

Given that statistic, it's little surprise that 67 percent of respondents reported taking their business elsewhere as a result of shoddy service during the previous year. The estimated average value, in U.S. dollars, that each of those defectors took with them each time they switched companies? About $4,000.

There are a number of explanations for why service expectations are rising around the globe. As more service-savvy companies expand their tentacles into emerging markets and more businesses sell products and services over the Web, customers in developing countries are exposed to what quality service feels like. Anyone in Brazil, India, or Zambia who's done business with FedEx, Amazon.com, Netflix, or Zappos.com, for example, is more likely to expect that same level of customer care from the next company they deal with, regardless of whether it's the mom-and-pop restaurant or auto repair shop around the corner.

Organizations also are realizing that today it's harder than ever to get away with bad service. Offend customers or give them robotic or indifferent treatment and the odds are high that the experience will be retold in vivid detail on the Web or on social networks. And if a customer's horrific service experience gets enough attention on a site like YouTube or Twitter, the traditional media will often come calling for follow-up reports, which ratchets up the exposure.

The real fear of negative service experiences "going viral" is keeping more organizations honest, leading them to enhance their service quality to avoid the odds of negative publicity. That in turn leads customers to expect more of them and other companies they do business with, because the service bar has been raised.

Watchdogs of the Web: Are Social Networks Helping to Improve Service Quality?

The effect that the Web, blogs, and social networks are having on companies' service performance might be compared to the influence that videocams and cell phone cameras have had on the actions of criminals and law enforcement officers. Both of these groups now know that the odds of their being caught on camera doing anything unlawful or ethically questionable have risen dramatically. Countless criminals (or unknowing celebrities—can anyone say Tiger Woods?) have had their acts caught by cell phone cameras, and police officers have been more wary of their public actions since the infamous Rodney King beating was caught on tape in the early 1990s.

Just as the prospect of being filmed has had a chilling effect on some parts of society, the knowledge that customers hold the ultimate megaphone in the form of the Internet should make companies more wary of providing poor service. Fair or not, if a customer feels as though he's been treated unjustly by your organization—especially if he senses that a legitimate complaint wasn't taken seriously—it's now reasonable to think you can expect thousands, even millions,

(continued)

(*Continued*)

of people to be reading about his experience quite soon on the Web.

That alone should be reason enough to ensure that you have the policies, training, and performance incentives in place to ensure that customers receive consistently high-quality service from your organization.

We use the equation *Expectation* × *Experience* = *Evaluation* to capture the process customers use to measure service performance. Expectations are what customers are *promised* as well as what is *expected*. For example, a doctor's office may promise prompt and attentive service, but what we expect might be different from that. The *Experience* is the outcome received and the process experienced. We might get the product we wanted at a fair price, but the process of finding or buying it might have been so cumbersome (consider a maddeningly slow or complex ordering process on a web site) as to create a different perception of the experience. The *Evaluation*, of course, is the customer's appraisal of the transaction based on Expectations multiplied by Experience.

Expectations are a function of customers' accumulated service experiences—regardless of where those experiences have occurred. Consider the customer who walks into a home improvement store desperately seeking a replacement part for the garbage disposal she began installing that morning. Rather than making her walk back and forth around the cavernous store to find some assistance, an observant apron-clad employee senses her urgency, approaches her, listens to her dilemma, and proceeds to walk her right to the exact part she needs. Not only that, but tapping into his own experience with installing garbage disposals, the clerk gives the customer some tips on how to install the part. The end result: a very happy customer who is in and out of the store in less than 30 minutes.

What do you think that customer's expectation will be the next time she encounters a similar situation, whether in an electronics store, a bank, or a pizza parlor? That's right—she'll likely expect the service staff to match the level of care and attention she received from the home improvement business. Customers who even occasionally do business with service exemplars such as Netflix, Zappos.com, L. L. Bean, JetBlue Airways, or Amazon.com don't suddenly abandon their high expectations when they visit their local grocer, DVD rental shop, or flower store. Rather, they usually think, *If that company can provide consistently good service, why can't you?*

Fair or not, each time customers walk away impressed by another company's service, it influences their decision on whether to keep doing business with you. Each experience, whether online or in the bricks-and-mortar world, resets expectations for the next encounter. That concept is worth pondering. A customer logs on to Amazon.com to get an update on the status of her product shipment. Then she calls or e-mails your web site for a similar update. If you're not as efficient and friendly as Amazon.com, you lose.

The Customer Experience Grid

Of course, knowing that customers have expectations and figuring out those expectations are two different things. Some are obvious: "I'd like a response to my e-mail by the end of the business day." Others are more unrealistic: "The product was delivered a day late. I think a new flat-screen TV would be fair atonement for the inconvenience I experienced."

To be able to accommodate as many expectations as possible, you first need to know how to find them. A model that we use to describe the sum total of customers' experiences is called the Customer Experience Grid. (See Figure 1.1.)

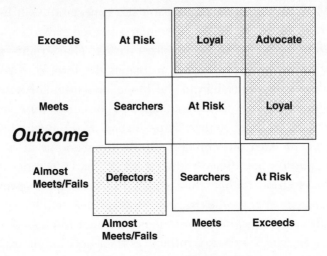

Figure 1.1   The Customer Experience Grid

The vertical axis of the grid is the *outcome* the customer receives, indicating whether it exceeds, meets, or almost meets/fails expectations. That outcome could be a product ordered from a web site, a meal delivered in a restaurant, or the experience in a dentist's office. In other words, the outcome is whatever your core offering is to the customer.

The horizontal axis is the *process* the customer has to go through to obtain that outcome. It's how easy it is to find price information on a web site, how long diners have to wait for their meal, how many calls have to be made to get a service problem resolved. It is on *process* dimensions where most companies have a chance to differentiate themselves and make impressions that keep customers coming back again and again.

Failing to meet customer needs on both process and outcome dimensions means that they probably won't darken your doorstep again; these are the *Defectors* on the grid. With all the other options that exist today, these customers are unlikely to give your organization a second chance. If a customer's needs are met in one dimension but not another—if the outcome was acceptable but the process to get there was like a poke in the eye—they'll also be actively looking to replace you. Their message to you is this: "I'm still on board, but I'm looking for someone else who can more consistently meet my needs." These are what we call the *Searchers*.

Then there are those who are *At Risk*, which is the middle band on the grid. They have what we call *commercial attention deficit disorder* (CADD) because you've given them very little reason to be loyal to you. A series of failings on the process or outcome sides makes them highly vulnerable to the gravitational pull of your competitors—thus the reason for their lack of attention to you. You might have met their outcome needs—perhaps your web site carries the style and size of shoes they've been desperately searching for—but something about the online ordering process was so burdensome that they abandoned their shopping cart before finishing. So you might have a great product offering, but if you combine it with poorly designed, incompetent, or uncaring service, you have an "at-risk" customer.

Another band is the *Loyal* customer, created when you meet expectations on one level and exceed them on another. These people, although perhaps not outspoken evangelists for your organization, are perfectly content keeping their business with you. They have little reason to look elsewhere. And, because they like you, they are willing to help you improve by offering ideas, changes, or suggestions.

But who you are really seeking—an organization's most valuable asset—is the *Advocate*, a customer who will talk up the great products or service your company offers with unrivaled passion. Advocates regularly have their expectations exceeded on both outcome and process measures. These are the people you find in chat rooms, on social networks, or at cocktail parties who gush about your organization and the amazing service they received.

The best part about Advocates: Their passionate word-of-mouth advertising doesn't cost you a nickel.

Speed as a Competitive Advantage

Customer expectations also are tied to a perception of the Internet as an almost instantaneous medium. Let's face it: When we "tweet," make a post to Facebook, or fire off an angry e-mail to a company, our expectation—rightly or wrongly—is that we'll get an almost immediate response. That's the nature of cyberspace and our "need it now" culture, a reality that makes speed of response an increasingly important service dimension in customers' minds.

In Accenture's global survey of customer satisfaction trends, respondents reported that fast resolution of their problems was the second most important factor in determining their overall satisfaction. In importance, that factor trailed only an ability to resolve issues by speaking to a single service representative rather than being forwarded to others—another issue that involves speed.

When customers see everything else as being equal—price, product quality, breadth of selection—how quickly you resolve their problems, answer their e-mails, or deliver Web-purchased products to their doorsteps can separate you from the pack.

Zappos.com, the online shoe retailer known for its superb customer service, believes the speed at which customers receive purchases made on the Web plays a critical role in their future loyalty. As a result, Zappos' top managers make delivery speed a top operational priority, opting to warehouse all the shoes the company sells. Unlike other online retailers, Zappos doesn't make an item available for sale unless it is physically present in one of its warehouses. That's because management knows the combination of quality shoe selection and speed of delivery is an unbeatable formula for binding customers to the company.

The Domino's pizza saga, detailed earlier in the chapter, offers another lesson in the importance of speed—in this case, how a lack of it can make an injury to a corporate reputation fester and grow. The prank video that the two Domino's employees posted on YouTube, which showed them doing untoward things with sandwiches, lingered on that popular site long enough to get over a million hits. Even more would have seen and been influenced by it had Domino's not been alerted to its presence by a blogger.

Had Domino's acted with greater speed, perhaps with the help of service staff dedicated to actively monitoring social media sites and the Web for any references to its products or brand, it might have been able to remove the video faster and better contain the damage. Never has the saying "You snooze, you lose" had more relevance than in the age of social media.

Even service exemplars like Amazon.com have learned painful lessons about customers' new service expectations surrounding speed. The company was forced to apologize after some members of Twitter complained about the sales rankings for gay and lesbian books mysteriously disappearing from the online retailer's site. Because Amazon took more than a day to respond to these complaints, the social media world criticized the company for being asleep at the wheel. Again, fair or not, that criticism reflects shifting expectations of how quickly customers believe companies should respond to problems in today's business environment, given new technologies and online networks.

E-Mail Versus Phone: Which Is Speedier?

There's also a common belief in organizations that e-mail provides customers with a faster way to interact than phone contact. Rather than wait on hold or wade through lengthy voice-mail menus, the thinking goes, customers can just shoot off an e-mail detailing their problems or questions and await a response. But the ability to solve problems faster via e-mail is largely a myth, particularly when problems are complex in nature.

Consider how much information and immediate problem solving can be packed into a 15-minute phone conversation with a company's service representative than in five back-and-forth e-mail exchanges that might happen over the course of three days. Experienced service professionals will tell you that inbound customer e-mails rarely contain all the information or detail necessary to solve the problem with one return e-mail.

While e-mail does provide a valuable paper trail for service interactions, when there is a need for speed and a more hassle-free way of resolving vexing problems in one contact, the phone usually wins out.

It pays to remember that customers are constantly comparing how easy it is to do business with you versus your competitors. If you can serve them faster or make them jump through fewer hoops than the other guy—while also providing quality product at competitive prices—they'll have little reason to spend their money elsewhere. Time is a highly prized commodity among today's global consumers. Whether it's a busy dual-income couple with children, a single person working 70 hour weeks, or a retiree anxious to wrap up his business so he can make his golf tee time, people increasingly want what's convenient, easy, and fast.

Give that to them on a consistent basis and you'll likely create customers for life.

More Educated Global Customers

Listening to the voice of today's customer also is crucial because consumers are more educated than ever before. Today the odds are greater than ever that customers have as much—or more—information about your products and services as your salespeople or customer service representatives. With the vast amount of information available on the Web, customers can price shop, access independent studies, check product reliability histories, or get comparative performance data at the click of a mouse. As more people in the developing world get high-speed Internet access, that consumer knowledge will only grow. All of which means that if your service staff doesn't have the latest-and-greatest knowledge about its own products and services as well as those of competitors, they risk being stumped by customers, which can be a death knell for their willingness to spend money with you. One study from the retailing world reported that customers identify salespeople "who know less about their products than I do" as a leading reason for switching from shopping at department stores to shopping via web sites.

It also means that the old-fashioned hard sell, long based on an assumption that companies have the upper hand on customers simply because they possess more knowledge about their products or services, is an increasingly bankrupt tactic in this age of the educated global consumer. On balance, more of today's customers prefer to do their own research on products or services rather than rely on a salesperson's efforts to convince them why they should spend their money with his organization rather than the competition.

Listening and responding to customers' distinct needs also takes on a new flavor as more companies do business around the world, including making inroads into emerging markets. Serving customers from different cultures requires an understanding of the unique values, expectations, and cultural norms people from other parts of the world bring to service interactions. If U.S.-based call center reps are too chatty with customers from Germany or use a first name before invited to do so, those customers can consider the informality disrespectful. Be too businesslike or avoid small talk with customers from Italy or France and they might consider it rude. Use too much direct eye contact with some customers in the Pacific Rim and they may be offended. Or use figures of speech or slang with customers not familiar with American idioms and they may go away more confused or alarmed than when they called in with a difficult service problem in the first place.

Educating your service staff about different cultural norms and expectations will keep them from "stepping in it" as they inevitably begin to deal with more customers from far corners of the world.

Five Building Blocks of Service Quality

Creating loyal customers also means understanding the foundational elements of service quality that are most important to them. There are five such "building blocks" of customer service that, executed well on a consistent basis, can turn lukewarm customers into passionate advocates. These RATER factors, created by service researcher Leonard Berry and colleagues at Texas A&M University, are *Reliability, Assurance, Tangibles, Empathy, and Responsiveness.*

Reliability

Reliability simply means doing what we say we're going to do for customers. Although this sounds easy in theory, "keeping the service promise" is where many companies slip up, leading to mistrust and causing customers to begin looking for greener pastures. Reliability, more than any other building block, is where customer loyalty is either cemented or fractured.

Reliability means serving a hot meal while it's still hot, processing orders that are accurate so that shipping can also be done in an accurate and efficient manner, and answering the switchboard calls promptly at 8:00 rather than 8:07. It's living up to your organization's marketing promises to deliver excellent service in each encounter.

Reliability has three components: organizational commitments, common expectations, and personal promises.

Organizational commitments. Companies make promises to their customers through advertising and marketing messages, service guarantees, and corporate correspondence. If you say you're going to provide "exceptional service, every time," provide delivery by 10:30 the next morning, or offer no longer than a five-minute wait in a bank queue, be prepared for customers to hold you to those promises. And for them to walk away sorely disappointed if you've raised their expectations, only to fall short in the end. For customers, making lofty promises about service quality and then not meeting them is tantamount to intentional bait and switch.

Common expectations. Based on their previous experience with you and other organizations, customers make assumptions about the quality of service they can expect from you. They might believe they can get a response to e-mail in two hours, have any problems resolved in one phone call, be greeted by name, or receive a tasty meal in under five minutes. Failing to meet these expectations is the same as breaking any other kind of promise.

Employees' personal promises. These are the promises your service staff makes every day, from promising to return a phone call by the end of the day to guaranteeing they'll show up for the plumbing job at the appointed hour or assuring customers that their cable bill won't increase for a full year.

Setting realistic expectations, then delivering on your promises—without fail—is the easiest way to set yourself apart from competitors who don't see the service promise as sacrosanct. Keeping the promises you make, and only making promises you can keep, is what reliability is all about.

Assurance

Being polite and upbeat with customers is an essential part of service delivery. But absent competence and confidence, a cheery attitude alone will do little to satisfy demanding customers. Consider the service technician who answers your call with an appealing, energetic phone voice, makes engaging small talk, but then just can't seem to figure out how to rid your computer operating system of a damaging virus. In such situations we usually just want the problem fixed post-haste, happy talk or not.

Customers need to be assured that they are dealing with a competent, well-trained, and knowledgeable representative of the company. Thanks to vast amounts of information on the Web, customers are more educated than ever before, and they quickly know if they're dealing with a crackerjack salesperson or call center rep who knows their products and services backward and forward—and how they stack up relative to the competition. People want to know that they are in good hands and that their issues will be handled with ease and competence.

When it comes to paying attention to customer needs, you *assure* them by listening attentively to what they are saying, repeating back or paraphrasing as needed for clarification, and then asking pertinent questions to ensure that a situation, experience, or point of view is understood. People don't want to have to repeat their problems—or worse, have to contact you again because you didn't listen well the first time. Listening well assures customers that their concerns are taken seriously and will be addressed in satisfactory fashion.

How you look, talk, make eye contact, listen, and respond to e-mail, Twitter posts, or instant messages all send a message to customers. Make sure that message states loud and clear: "I'm a competent, knowledgeable, and caring service professional."

Tangibles

This fundamental of the Pay Attention strategy focuses on how *tangibles* influence customer perception of service quality. Tangibles can include everything from a company's advertising to the cleanliness of a store to the attire of service professionals. All of the things, whether prominent or miniscule, that customers see, hear, smell, taste, or touch, affect their perception of your organization and the lengths to which you've gone to meet their service needs.

If a delivered product arrives in a damaged package, a parking lot is littered with trash, a business sign is unlit, a counter is sticky,

call center representatives use poor grammar, or you fail to provide confirmation of incoming e-mail, it can adversely influence
customers' willingness to do business with you again.

Remember: Tangibles help convey the value of the service
transaction's intangible aspects. Ignore or downplay them at your
own risk.

Empathy

Nothing destroys your customer satisfaction ratings—not to mention future customer loyalty—like treating customers as though
they're a number, a nuisance, or guilty before proven innocent.
The ability to show *empathy* for customers, particularly when they
feel they've been wronged, is a critical component of the Pay
Attention approach.

It's important to remember that empathy isn't the same as
sympathy, however. *Sympathy* involves identifying with, and even
taking on, your customers' emotions, as in "Frankly, I'm really
disappointed as well with our company's policy on this issue."
Empathy involves acknowledging and affirming another's emotional state, without taking it on yourself. For example, "I can
hear that you're angry that the product didn't arrive on time."

The distinction is important, because responding to customers
with sympathy all day can leave you emotionally drained and can
even make you more prone to siding with the customer against
your own organization. The key is being emotionally *in tune* without becoming too *involved*. Service professionals who respond
with empathy remain in control of their emotions while still communicating they understand the customer's feelings and point
of view.

In this day and age of endless voice-mail menus and cost-
obsessed companies that promote self-service or e-mail contact
options over 800-number phone service, providing a human-level
connection—a live, empathetic voice to talk to—can make a lasting impression on customers just by virtue of its rarity. Netflix

is among the companies that understand that phone-based customer service, though more expensive than other options, can pay huge dividends in terms of customer loyalty (which translates to a big reduction in marketing dollars needed to attract customers that replace unhappy ones who have defected) by providing an oasis of humanity and one-stop service efficiency in a business world too often marked by companies that erect automated contact "moats" to keep customers at bay.

Responsiveness

Quick, efficient action has always been the hallmark of good service, and never more so than in the social media age. Customers have come to expect rapid response to their e-mail or Twitter posts about service problems, next-morning delivery of vital business documents, eyeglasses made in one hour, instant answers to Google queries, and their grande lattes handed out the drive-thru window in just minutes.

But not every service issue needs to be solved in nanoseconds. There's a big difference between a customer who needs a suit with a nasty coffee stain cleaned ASAP for a big presentation the next morning and someone who brings a dry cleaner seasonal clothes that don't need attention for weeks. It's important to talk to your customers to determine what they deem acceptable waits or service response times. According to a study conducted by the National Restaurant Association, "fast" service for customers of fast-food restaurants means five minutes or less, whereas diners in a sit-down family restaurant are willing to wait as long as 30 minutes for their meals to arrive. Similarly, customers might exhibit more patience in getting their double mocha latte and scone on a lazy Saturday morning than during the Monday morning rush hour.

Responsiveness is also about keeping customers apprised of problems that arise. Think being proactive, not reactive. Consider passengers stewing in their airplane seats as their scheduled departure time comes and goes. Kept in the dark about reasons for the delay, their frustration will build and their imaginations perhaps get the best of them. But if the captain comes over the intercom to apologize and explain reasons for the delay, whether weather, airport traffic logjams, or a mechanical issue, passengers at least have some information to work with. In face-to-face service situations, simply acknowledging your customer with eye contact or a polite "Sorry for the wait—I'll be with you as soon as I can" goes a long way toward slowing the steam emerging from a customer's ears.

It's also important to remind your service staff that although deadlines are important, they *do* have some control over setting them. If someone tells a customer they'll have an answer in two hours, they're creating an expectation for the client and setting a deadline for themselves. In that sense it's important to be realistic with estimates—when in doubt, give yourself more time than less—because deadlines become the yardstick by which customers measure your success or failure.

Chapter 2

PAY ATTENTION TO YOUR MARKETING MESSAGE

Today's customers require a different marketing approach than we have seen in the past. Historically, organizations were able to finely tune their marketing messages with skill and precision. They had time to determine slogans, advertisements, and key demographics used in newspapers, direct mail, TV, or other mass media. In short, they had control of their brand images.

Those days are largely behind us. Today, with all the new communication tools available to consumers—blogs, third-party social networks, customer review sites, YouTube, and the like—people receive messages about your organization in record time, whether you're ready to unveil those messages or not. This possibly happens even faster than you can react.

Bloggers, social networkers, and other Web users are constantly sharing experiences or exchanging opinions about the quality of your products or services. These consumers have in effect wrested a large measure of control from your marketing department by influencing how your brand is perceived by untold millions around the globe.

Participating versus Observing

So what does this shift—a change likely to persist beyond the life spans of specific services such as Facebook, Twitter, My-Space, or LinkedIn—mean for the way you market and sell to customers?

Marketing experts today suggest a bigger focus on *participative* marketing, an approach that requires involving your customers. The difference between participative marketing and traditional marketing is that you're not pushing your message *at* your customer; rather, you are engaging your customer to work *with* you. Embracing this change comes down to answering a simple question: Will you allow potentially millions of consumers to shape the perception of your company without your participation, or will you actively engage with and listen to them in an attempt to influence how they view your organization—and your service quality?

Participative marketing also means rethinking old mindsets about effective sales approaches. As Albert Maruggi, head of Provident Partners, a marketing consulting firm in St. Paul, Minnesota, says of social media marketing: "It's about telling, not selling." This telling occurs in the sense of educating communities of like-minded customers about what your organization has to offer, not simply targeting a demographic by age or ZIP code. It's about using independent research, articles written by trusted news sources, and the opinions of credible peers to educate customers about your products and services, not just flood them with traditional marketing materials. It's about paying closer attention to what customers say or write about your company, then separating the baseless rants from thoughtful feedback and using the latter to enhance your service performance or product quality.

But using new marketing avenues such as social networks can backfire without having a sound business reason for doing so. Are you using Facebook and Twitter, for example, to simply increase brand awareness, measured in terms of online conversations, or to boost real sales, gauged by hard sales numbers? Either approach might suit your mission, but the important thing is to have a well-defined goal for marketing via these new tools beyond mere bandwagon jumping.

"It is not, 'We should be on Facebook!' but rather, 'Why should we be on Facebook and how will our daily routine change because of that decision?'" says Maruggi.

Fundamentals Are Still Key

This shift in focus doesn't diminish the foundational components of a good marketing strategy. The same principles that worked 25 years ago still apply; they simply need tweaking to appeal to today's fast-paced, increasingly skeptical, research-loving, perpetually Web-connected customers.

There are four components to an effective marketing strategy:
1. Pay attention to who you are—what's your purpose?
2. Pay attention to who your audience is.
3. Pay attention to engaging your customers.
4. Pay attention to walking your marketing talk.

Pay Attention to Who You Are

What do you want to be famous for? Why are you in business? What is it about your organization that makes customers want to spend their hard-earned money with you rather than your competitors? These are the questions that need answers before you can develop compelling marketing messages.

Burger Jones, a restaurant chain that recently opened in Minneapolis, was reviewed by *The Onion*, a newspaper known for its satire as well as its serious restaurant reviews:

> Consider the lowly hamburger. It's just two pieces of bread, a handful of ground beef, and maybe a pickle—nothing more, right? The newest entry into the meat-and-bun field is Burger Jones, a short-order, limited-menu pattie palace . . .
> —Carla Waldemar, *The Onion*

Now that's pretty clear, according to *The Onion*, at least: Burger Jones is all about mouth-watering burgers.

Or consider this from Parkson Corporation in Ft. Lauderdale, Florida:

> Parkson is a leader in the water and wastewater industry, and a leading provider of advanced solutions in water and wastewater recycling and treatment.

Again, no waffling or identity crisis here; Parkson is all about water.

And last, how about this from the Mall of America's Nickelodeon Universe in Bloomington, Minnesota:

> Nickelodeon Universe®, the nation's largest indoor family theme park . . . is home to seven acres of fun with more than 30 remarkable rides and attractions and, of course, shopping.

Nickelodeon Universe is clearly all about family fun.

What do these three statements have in common? They all clearly testify to what the business stands for. That doesn't just mean having a statement of purpose prominently displayed on a web site or place of business. What separates savvy marketers from their mediocre brethren is an ability to clearly communicate a purpose for being to every employee and every customer, internal or external. To have clarity of purpose for your organization, you'll need to answer a few basic but vital questions:

- Why is our organization in business?
- Who are we?
- What do we strive to achieve?
- What do customers want or expect from us, given what we communicate to them about our operations?

Another consideration is what makes you unique or how you stand apart from the other businesses in your niche. Let's return to the Burger Jones example. Guests are known to wait 45 minutes in line to sample one of these burgers. Why? What's the appeal? It's just a gosh-darn burger! How has Burger Jones achieved differentiation? The company uses only the finest blends of beef, cheeses, and other toppings. Burger Jones has chosen to focus on essentially one item and do it better than most. There's no chicken, no pork, no salads—it's a burger, and they've made that more than enough.

Another way organizations can differentiate themselves is through their speed of service. For example, Zappos.com is a recognized leader in the shipping and service end of the e-tailer category. Zappos customers know that a shoe order placed on a Monday will be received by Friday of that same week—*with no shipping cost*. The company takes that service one step further by offering free return shipping on all purchases.

Purchasing shoes without first trying them on can be a daunting prospect, but Zappos makes shopping on its web site stress-free and knows that once customers have ordered a pair of highly desired shoes, they don't want to wait any longer than necessary to receive them. And should those shoes not fit properly, they want to make product return as quick and painless as possible.

Other organizations might choose customer care, even pampering, as their competitive advantage. Ritz Carlton Hotels are legendary for the level of personal service they provide at their facilities, characterized by many little touches that delight customers. Hotel guests at a Ritz Carlton property have come to expect a standard of care far above the norm in the hotel industry—regardless of which property they're visiting. Ritz Carlton's service standards are consistent and true throughout the world, and the hotel's marketing approaches reflect that consistency.

In moving from e-mail-based to phone-based customer support, the DVD rental company Netflix is able to market its higher level of human touch—and customers' ability to get questions or problems resolved in one short phone call rather than a series of back-and-forth e-mail exchanges—in positioning itself against its competitors.

Finally, in answering the "Who are we?" question, organizations might opt to hang their hat on product innovation. Apple Computer, for example, has a history of developing breakthrough products. Whether the iPhone, iPod, Macbook, iPad, or something yet to be unveiled, Apple regularly lures new customers with creative product designs and features that support a brand image (and often, customers' own self-image) of being cutting-edge, hip, and a little outside the mainstream.

Regardless of how you decide to position your organization and whatever you choose as your competitive distinguisher, these factors must be integrated into everything you say and do.

Pay Attention to Who Your Audience Is

Today's consumers are a different breed. They are, on average, more educated, tuned in, "tweet-friendly," self-reliant, and influential than ever before. Given your overarching marketing purpose—finding and maintaining a clear competitive distinguisher—ask yourself the following questions about your customer base:

- Who do you envision as your audience?
- Who is currently buying and/or using your products or services?
- What are you doing to segment and analyze your customer base?
- Does the customer who is stopping in, trying out, or logging on look like the person you envisioned?

The answers to these questions could be as you expected, or they may surprise you. If they're what you anticipated, pat yourself on the back; you've profiled and segmented your customer base pretty well. But what if there are surprises? That's not necessarily a negative. It could be that your audience is much broader than you envisioned, which opens up new possibilities. Do a little more research and determine whether you've miscalculated or if you just need to enhance your marketing scope a bit.

There are a number of ways to assess who your existing—and potential—customers are:

- **Ask.** One on one, perhaps as a short follow-up to transactions handled over the phone, via e-mail, social networks, or face to face. Focus on how customers are using your product, where they are located, what other demographics are. Make a concerted effort to have salespeople, servers, or service support staff tally what they learn.
- **Survey.** Formally, at the time of inquiry or purchase. When you are wrapping up the sale online or in person, ask a couple of targeted questions to learn more.
- **Entice.** Offer some incentive for information. Provide customers with a bounce-back coupon, for example, for taking time to complete a short survey for demographic

purposes—kind of the "You scratch my back and I'll scratch yours" idea.

- **Observe.** You or your staff can watch customers in action, shopping for or using products or services. Certainly this is much more challenging when you are online. But when a live chat, tweet, or e-mail conversation ensues, it might be the perfect time to make some assessments.
- **Focus groups.** Volunteers provide feedback and insights in specific areas or topics. Maybe you've been in the mall and been approached to answer some questions. The Mall of America regularly sends associates into the mall to interact with small groups of customers to find out how their day is going, what makes the mall special to them, and what challenges they have encountered during their visit.
- **Online review.** Check key customer review sites such as Yelp.com to see who's writing about you and what the reviewers' demographics are, as well as assessing comments left on your own web site. There are any number of ways to make this task easy. We offer more detail on this approach in Chapter 5.

Once you've gathered data, analyze it against who you believe to be your core and secondary audience. Ask yourself how the data aligns with your beliefs. What market segments show strength? What market segments are missing? Where can we grow? Where should we possibly diminish our focus? Where might we be hurting ourselves by trying to be all things to all people?

There's another factor that makes today's customers unique: A desire for control. On one level, consumers have more control than ever over how your brand is perceived by others, given the growth of communication channels such as social networks, customer review sites, and blogs. With many millions accessing these tools every day and offering opinions on the quality of products or services they've used, consumer word of mouth—or *mouse*—marketing has grown more influential than ever.

On another level, the desire for control is reflected in the continued popularity of the do-it-yourself (DIY) industry, exemplified by TV channels such as HGTV or the Food Network and fueled by stores such as Lowe's and Home Depot that encourage homeowners to undertake their own remodeling or repair projects. TV shows abound on how to fix, make, build, repair, create, or flip just about anything you can think of—without the help of certified professionals.

Want more evidence of the DIY phenomenon? Search the Internet for options on buying a new or pre-owned car. Sites such as Edmunds.com or Vehix.com offer manufacturers' specifications, ratings, or pricing on any aspect of a vehicle. Shoppers can even compare multiple options on multiple vehicles at one time. It's as easy as type and click. If you want the scoop on how a vehicle performs before you buy it, owner reviews and repair frequency data abound; all you have to do is look for them.

In addition, more consumers are buying into local food coops to have fresher, in-season, lower carbon-impact food than ever before. The rise of the grow-it-yourself garden craze has also been sweeping the United States.

The upshot: There is clear evidence that today's consumers are more self-directed, less reliant on traditional marketing appeals, and more willing to do their own exhaustive research before making buying decisions.

The Power of Customer Stories

Where audience is concerned, the goal of any organization is to build a loyal and unwavering following. In Chapter 1 we examined the ways in which customers evaluate and assess service quality. When an organization exceeds expectations in evaluation and satisfaction dimensions, it begins to build all-important customer loyalty, and those "advocate" customers often tell wonderful stories about you. And marketing professionals will tell you there's nothing as persuasive—and cost-effective—as positive word-of-mouth advertising.

Research by our colleague, Dr. Chip Bell, suggests that customers are eager to share stories about the good service they receive. Those stories usually fall into one of three categories:

Category One: *"They have the most helpful employees."*

These stories have little to do with the quality of your products or services and much to do with the people who serve the customer.

Category Two: *"They help me make the right choice."*

These stories concern your products and services but also the knowledge, patience, and insight provided by staff in helping customers make buying decisions.

Category Three: *"They're really easy to do business with."*

These stories have to do with eliminating the "hassle" factor: how well you remove the typical headaches, hoops, or roadblocks customers face in conducting business with your organization. We explore this topic, what we call being ETDBW (easy to do business with), in more detail in Chapter 4.

Let's look at brief examples of each of these categories.

"They have the most helpful employees."

Maggie, a starving grad student, often orders clothing via the Web. The first time she ordered from Lands' End, she decided to keep some items and return others. In calling the 800 customer service number to ensure that she returned the items correctly, she was informed that if she had a Sears store in her area she could return the items to that location, thereby saving the shipping costs, and receive immediate credit. Thrilled with that option, Maggie explained that the Sears store nearby was a smaller store and didn't carry the Lands' End brand. Again, she was informed that made no difference. Maggie was delighted with the time and cost savings the service representative provided, delivered in a cheerful and efficient manner to boot.

In this situation, the representative listened carefully to the questions and implied concerns of the customer. Surmising that immediate credit might be helpful and hearing that special sizing was a concern, she reassured the customer that a return to the local Sears store would still work for her and expedite credit on her account. By being proactive and helpful, the service rep ultimately exceeded Maggie's expectations and made her eager to share the service story with friends, family, and others.

Bottom line: It's important that your frontline associates have the right attitude and skills to do the job. Making the personal connection with each customer points out how well they Pay Attention!

"They help me make the right choice."

In planning for a tour through several parts of Europe, some friends of ours decided they wanted to travel light. This required only a backpack and small carry-on bag to facilitate ease of travel. In preparation for the purchase of the backpacks, the travelers did extensive research on the Internet. They compared brands, reviewed customer feedback, and checked prices. Finally deciding on a vendor, the travelers made a phone call to the customer service/sales group to discuss their selection.

Through a series of questions and discussion, a service representative determined that a change in size of the backpack for one of the travelers would be critical. "Since one of you is short and petite in build, I'm concerned that your choice will prove very uncomfortable over the course of your trip," he advised. Grateful to learn more about the packs' balance and weighting issues, our friends made changes to their initial selections based on expert recommendations and were more confident in their purchase. Needless to say, the recommendations of the customer service expert paid off and they had a wonderful trip.

Here we see a knowledgeable associate taking the time to engage the customer and make a real connection. The customer was wowed by the support, advice, and guidance and took the recommendations to heart. By making a human connection and providing shrewd advice, the rep created customers who were anxious to spread the word far and wide about the memorable service they received.

"They're really easy to do business with."

Here's a story with an interesting twist that a friend of ours, Ellie, sent to us.

"I went to a Macy's store in downtown St. Paul to purchase a bridal shower gift from their bridal registry. The associate reviewed the registry list that I had just printed and pointed me in the general direction of where various items were located in the store. There were no other customers in the department at the time. So I asked the clerk if he could help me find specific items, since he would be familiar with his inventory. He reluctantly agreed to help and did so.

"I decided on the item I was going to buy, then purchased it and asked where the gift wrap department was located. He replied that the St. Paul store no longer offers a gift-wrapping service because they were losing money on it. I suggested that even if that's the case, they should offer something as a service to their customers, even if they have gift wrapping their customers could purchase. He showed me their limited selection and then suggested that I notify Macy's corporate office on my own to ask them to reinstate the service. He then pointed me in the general direction of a Hallmark store nearby so I could purchase the materials I needed elsewhere."

Who did all the work in this situation? Do you think Ellie will go rushing back to do business with that store again, where getting even a minimum level of help was akin to pulling teeth? Regardless of the economy, regardless of the size of the purchase, it is in your best interest to make it easy for customers to do business with you.

In cases like this it's important to remember how easy it is for today's customers to spread the word about negative service experiences—whether over the back fence to their neighbors, on a blog, in a tweet, in a YouTube video, a Facebook post, a review at Yelp.com, or countless other online avenues. Study your operational processes and service policies from the customer's point of view—from the outside looking in. Think about what the customer is experiencing, the hoops you're making them jump through to do business with you. It's from that analysis that you can make changes that ensure that customers look forward to spending their money with you, not dread the prospect of walking through your doors or clicking onto your web site.

Pay Attention to Engaging Your Customers

Once you're clear about who you are and what makes you unique, the next challenge is getting the message out. One of the best ways to do that is to engage your customers in places where they congregate, whether online or in the bricks-and-mortar world.

For many companies, that means creating a bigger marketing presence on social media channels such as Twitter, Facebook, YouTube, and more. Though some remain skeptical of putting marketing resources into these networks, compelling data shows that being deeply engaged in social media has a correlation to improved financial performance. Two research groups, the Altimeter Group and Wetpaint, joined forces to study how the 100 most valuable brands, as defined by the 2008 Business Week/Interbrand Best Global Brands ranking, engaged in 11 different online social media channels. The brands were critiqued not only on the breadth of their engagement across social media but also on their depth, meaning whether they do things such as reply to comments made on blog posts.

Companies with the greatest breadth and depth were dubbed social media mavens. The study's authors found that these mavens, on average, grew their revenues by 18 percent over the 12-month period studied, compared to the least engaged companies, which, on average, saw a decline of 6 percent in revenue in the same period.

The authors stress that they're not claiming a causal relationship but clearly a strong correlation. What's their theory for the improved financial performance of the mavens? "A mindset that allows a company to broadly engage with customers on the whole probably performs better because the company is more focused on its customers than the competition," they write.

Here are some specific examples of how companies are engaging customers on social media with marketing appeals:

- Dell Computer uses Twitter to post tweets alerting customers to sales and new products as well as to the arrival of refurbished computers to its Dell Outlet store. Dell does a lot of micro blogging, with some 20-plus accounts on Twitter. It also uses Twitter for loyalty marketing. In exchange for following Dell Outlet's Twitter account, for example, tweeters in the United States get access to exclusive deals not available outside Twitter.

- The Dozen Bake Shop in Lawrence, Pennsylvania, announces daily specials or newly introduced scones, cakes, and other items on its Facebook page. The small business has more than 600 Facebook fans and 400 Twitter followers who read these posts religiously.

- The Mall of America is using a YouTube video to attract candidates for job openings. The thinking is that this is one of the best mediums to target the audience the mall is after.

- Southwest Airlines features key marketing messages and promotions on YouTube, Facebook, and Twitter. You can live the life of a Southwest employee or see an airplane assembled on these channels.

- On its corporate web site, Starbucks offers the My Starbucks Idea option, asking customers or employees to post their best ideas for product or service improvements, check out others' ideas and vote on which they like, discuss ideas to make them better, and see which ideas Starbucks actually adopted.

- Even the ultra-traditional brand Burberry has announced a new social networking site to encourage customers to post their own trench coat stories. Reaching out to a younger, trendier audience is a significant move for the brand. Burberry currently has 699,000 fans on Facebook and is attracting customers via Twitter and YouTube.

Rancho Bernardo Inn
Hotel Makes Creative Use of Twitter to Entice Guests

Realizing that many travelers were canceling or altering vacation plans during the recent economic downturn, the Rancho Bernardo Inn, a luxury resort located in San Diego, decided to get creative and offer its guests a special Survivor Package. The inn also turned to Twitter to advertise many other unique discounted deals.

The base rate for a deluxe room and breakfast for two at the inn is $219 per night. However, under the Survivor Package, guests could choose to eliminate certain amenities from their rooms and lower the rate accordingly.

Here's the discount chart:
- $199 without breakfast
- $179 without honor bar
- $159 without A/C or heat
- $139 without pillows
- $109 without sheets
- $89 without lights
- $59 without linens
- $39 without toiletries
- $19 without bed

(continued)

(*Continued*)

John Gates, the hotel's general manager, said that roughly 25% of guests participating in the Survivor Package were opting for the $19 option.[1] The special offer was available for only a month, and all available rooms quickly sold out.

The Survivor offering isn't the only example of Gates' inventive marketing approach. He's also had good success using Twitter to post unique and often quirky deals to entice guests in a difficult market. Here is a sampling of some of the offers GMGoneMad (a.k.a. John Gates' Twitter account) has made:

- We still have rooms this wknd. Call 2 arrange a stay. Show up w/ cxl'd reservation from another property and receive 50% discount off room rate.
- Cleaning up after busy wknd. Up 4 a challenge? Who can make bed the fastest? You vs. room attendant using only 1 hand. Win free room nite.
- Wknd vry busy—full property w/ 3 weddings. Parking an issue—no room. Still wnt yr $$ though, so ride a bike, we'll give U 50% off meal.
- 2 VIP pets at RBI??? Bring in an untraditional under-50 lb pet & we'll pet sit while you dine in one of our restaurants—this weekend only!
- We have room in our award-winning Mother's Day brunch, bring in your own eggs and we'll sell you a room for $119 Saturday night.
- Happy Monday, full Resort today :) And my daughter's birthday. Anyone bring in a cake, receive free dinner for two in Veranda tonight.
- Hot weekend in So Cal. First guest to pull up in vehicle that doesn't have AC wins free gift cert for a stay—as we have AC (and 3 pools) :)

> - May Day tomorrow. Anyone know the tradition? Bring a flower to front desk and receive 50% off your entire weekend stay! Valid 5/1-5/10
>
> Asked about response to the Twitter offers, Gates confirms that "Yes, folks are taking action on our offers. We've generally gotten two to three bookings per tweet. Glad you enjoy them!"

Larry Huston, vice president of innovation at consumer products company Procter & Gamble, says that "successful brands have a story that consumers tell themselves when they reach for the product in the store to buy it." Customers see themselves enjoying, using, and engaged with your product or service and often see their choice as a reflection of their own personalities—or what they hope to become. With clarity of purpose, it will be easier to customize that message for each person.

In addition to considering the best strategies for a participative marketing plan, it can be helpful to revisit the classic "4 P's" of an effective marketing mix, first introduced by marketing guru E. J. McCarthy.

Product. Historically the thinking has been that a good product will sell itself. With today's increased competition, that's no longer a given. Now businesses should ask: Does the product create what its intended audience wants? Companies must define the characteristics of their products or services that meet the unique needs of their audience. A good starting point is to ask, How does this product or service benefit my customer better than the competition's offerings? How does it make their operations more efficient, their life easier or more enjoyable in some way?

Place. Place is a moving target. Certainly, if you're a bricks-and-mortar operation, location can make all the difference. You only have to live with construction woes for a short time before realizing what an impact location can have on your business.

Conversely, one of the benefits of e-commerce is that your business could be located almost anywhere. But the downside is that people can't just "wander by" and stop in if they're passing by on their lunch break or on their way home from work. That's why mastering search engine optimization (SEO) and other online marketing tactics is so vital for luring customers to your web site. Regardless of your location and type of business—whether clicks or bricks—you have to figure out the best ways to let your audience know where you are and how they can best access your products or services.

Price. Pricing should be a very conscious decision. Competing on price alone has put some of the best companies out of business. In one of our service seminars, a field service engineer handed us this quote: "Anyone can beat you on price. It's your service that sets you apart." Indeed. Even your employees know that price alone is, over time, a weak differentiator. So if your employees know this, it goes without saying that your customers also know.

What are you doing to make yourself stand apart in a market rife with me-too products and nondescript customer service?

Promotion. How do all the segments of your customer base know about the products and services you have available? Pay attention to all aspects of engagement—advertising, sales, marketing, public relations—delivered via print, direct mail, Web, social networking sites, blogs, podcasts, or user-generated video sites. Word-of-mouth marketing is more valuable than ever, given the ability of positive (or negative) service experiences to travel across the oceans at the click of a mouse. We believe this "P" is the most important component of all in today's global market.

It's through in-person service transactions and online conversations that you build connections with customers, and from those connections you find the opportunities to *engage* them. McCarthy defines engagement as "a series of interactions that strengthens a customer's emotional connection to the product or firm."

When customers envision themselves using, holding, or integrating your product or service, there is a stronger emotional connection. When you prove to them, time and again, that you have their best interests at heart—when you truly listen to customers and resolve their problems cheerfully and efficiently—they build emotional bonds to you. And that makes it harder for competitors to pry them away with lower prices or shiny new product features.

Learn how customers perceive using your products or services. Does the experience convey warmth? Joy? Excitement? Fear? Frustration? Safety? Intelligence?

To help you better figure this out, consider some of the following:

- What is the frequency of purchase? Is this product something the customer will buy only once (a new home, a new car, the first prom dress) or repeatedly (breakfast cereal, lawn and garden tools, music downloads)?
- What is the frequency of interaction? Will the customer come back repeatedly (a restaurant, grocery store, special event location, special camping area)?
- What is the type of service interaction? Is it inquiry, involvement, engagement—passive or active?
- Where will the interaction occur? Does the customer connect with a person, a web site, via the telephone or a social networking site, in your space or theirs?
- What is the category of the interaction? Was the customer buying one core item, an add-on item, an additional category of merchandise or service?
- Is a reward or frequent buyer program offered? Does the customer have a card or number immediately ready, or do you have to look it up?
- Has the customer made a referral (an indication that they are a loyal or advocate customer)?

How you answer these questions should give you some insight into the breadth of your customer relationships and the level of customer engagement. Engagement is where it's at today. Marketing gurus encourage businesses to look at the level of engagement and how that connects to building customer relationships and loyalty. It's a whole new ball game.

Pay Attention to Walking Your Marketing Talk

Marketing in today's business climate also means taking extra steps to ensure congruency between what you *promise* and what you *deliver* to your customers. As we explored in Chapter 1, today's consumers are more skeptical of advertising and hard-sell marketing tactics than previous generations. Many prefer to research their options, talk to their peers, pore over independent studies, and do exhaustive price shopping rather than simply accept promised product or service advantages on their face.

Few things raise the ire of these customers faster than splashy marketing campaigns that promise "positively memorable service," "no longer than a five-minute wait, guaranteed," or "no-hassle product returns" only to discover, once they've done business with the organization, that the slogans are little more than empty promises—or worse, bait-and-switch tactics. Better not to promise service excellence in any form than to raise customer hopes and then dash them on the shores of indifferent, poorly resourced, or overly automated customer service.

Customers today know and react to the consistency—or lack thereof—between what you say and what you do. All you need do is visit popular customer review web sites such as Yelp to see how frequently users comment on the chasm between what companies promise and the product or service quality the customers actually receive.

Don't Promise Great Service If You Can't Deliver

Indeed, many organizations learn the hard way about making service promises in marketing campaigns that their service staff isn't prepared to deliver on. In a blog post, Deborah Chaddock Brown, editor of the customer service newsletter *Words People Read*, detailed an experience with a bank that underscores the importance of managing customer expectations and of avoiding raising customer hopes if performance can't match advertising boasts.

> Writes Brown: I just made a deposit at the drive-through window of my bank. When I pulled up to the magic tube that shoots up and over into the bank, I noticed a computerized screen that said, "Honk if you receive excellent customer service."
>
> Oh, I thought, they are focusing on customer service. I wonder what they will do that will inspire me to honk. Let's see—I have filled out the form, signed the back of my check, and placed a request for a little cash back. I sent the tube up and over and then waited to be astounded with their excellence.
>
> I measure excellence based on my expectations. In this case, I am expecting the check to be deposited and the little bit of cash to be returned to me. So that is my "line in the sand."
>
> The screen changes to reveal the face of the teller who is serving my needs and is sure to exceed them.
>
> "Hi," she says.
>
> "Hi," I mimic. Okay—get ready. My radar is up. The seeds of excellence have been planted.
>
> The screen changes back to the "honk" message. My hand is poised over the steering wheel.

(continued)

(*Continued*)

The screen changes again to the teller. "Thank you," she says.

Down comes the tube with my deposit receipt and cash. No lollypop. No special message. It is the Friday before a holiday—no special greeting to send me on my holiday-way.

Oh. Now I'm disappointed. Truth is, had there been no message about honking if you receive great service, I would have left quite pleased. I had my expectations met. No hassle. No issues. Made a deposit. Got some cash. Bada-bing, bada-boom.

But because there was a message that set the stage for excellence and just-average performance greeted me, I'm now leaving feeling deflated. Disappointed. Like I missed the parade.

Do we set expectations that we fail to meet? Truth is, I didn't need the message to complete my transaction. But because the seed was planted, I became more aware—a sense of expectation set in my mind, left unfulfilled.

Let me make a comparison. Last week I had my daughter and her friend in the car. We went through the drive-through of a different branch of the same bank. No special message. No computer screen. I sent the tube up and over and the teller did her job and as she was about to return the tube she asked me if my daughter would like a lolly. I said, "Oh yes, and she has a girlfriend in the back seat." Then the teller said, "Would you also like a lolly?" Why—yes, I would.

So here comes the tube with my deposit slip and three lollies. As we drove away my daughter's girlfriend said, "You should send her a thank-you note for being so nice."

Now *that's* excellence. A simple lolly. What do you think? Does your organization set the expectation for excellence and then frequently fail to produce, or do you set out to do what is expected and then throw in a little surprise? Which is more impactful?

Paying Attention to how you market to, and engage with, today's customers can pay big dividends. By expanding your reach to social media, you meet customers on turf where they're increasingly comfortable and receptive to doing business. And when you're clear about your purpose, about your company's competitive distinguisher, and about aligning the service quality you deliver with what you promise, you start to build trust—and a more loyal following.

Chapter 3

PAY ATTENTION TO PREPARATION

O f all the factors that contribute to shoddy customer service, the most overlooked may be a disconnect between management strategy and front-line employee actions. When executives profess that "service quality is goal #1" and plaster marketing campaigns, corporate correspondence, web sites, and wall posters with that new credo, employees with service mentalities naturally get fired up to start delivering on that promise.

But many times those lofty visions leave people with only a vague notion of how they should behave on the job in the name of delighting customers. How, for example, should they respond if they come upon negative rants about the company on social networks such as Facebook or customer review sites such as Yelp? What's an acceptable response time for answering tweets or e-mail sent by customers? What's the appropriate response to complaints made by gold-, silver-, or bronze-level customers?

Many service strategies also do little to help guide the hiring, training, compensation, and recognition practices essential to creating and sustaining a Pay Attention service culture. This is no small issue, because a service vision should be the lens through which your people view all of their decisions and actions to ensure that customers walk away from transactions thinking, "Now there's a company that really *gets it* about customer service."

Without a compelling service vision and well-defined service standards, the Pay Attention approach is missing the guide rails needed to keep your people on the right service path. And that absence can undermine service quality initiatives because, as the saying goes, *If you don't know where you're going, any road can take you there.*

The Power of Vision and Purpose

So, why do service strategies so often fall short of triggering service excellence on the front lines?

One of the biggest reasons is that they begin and end with mere exhortation on the part of senior managers. Too often leaders fail to follow up on bold statements of "creating positively exuberant customers" by also creating concrete strategies, standards, and norms that help workers understand what service quality should look like each day when they interact with customers in the trenches.

What it takes to create award-winning service might be clear in the CEO's mind, but until everyone on the front line understands it on the same visceral level, it does the organization little good. As Horst Schulze, former president of Ritz Carlton Hotels and current chairman, and president and CEO of The West Paces Hotel Group, was known to say, "Employees shouldn't be expected to deliver first-rate service if management can't first define it."

That starts with an effective and believable *service vision statement.* The statement should contain a detailed profile of your core customer base, describe what you do that sets you apart from competitors, and outline how you—and your customers—will know when the goal of customer delight is achieved. The statement, and its supporting standards, should be so well defined that your people never hesitate over which side to come down on when faced with a vexing service scenario. It should ensure that everyone in your business unit operates with the same shared concept of "what's important around here."

Both reliability, the attribute detailed in Chapter 1 that customers repeatedly cite as the most important factor in determining their loyalty, and consistent delivery of service quality flow from good service vision statements. Not surprisingly, there is a strong correlation between compelling service strategies and customer satisfaction rankings. Our research unearthed some telling statistics when it comes to the power of good service visions:

- If you do not have a definition of what good service means, you have about a 30 percent chance of getting high marks from your customers.
- If you have a very general definition, your chances of getting high marks from customers are 50/50.
- If you have a detailed definition of what good service means—if it is defined within the context of the company and the customer, if it is well communicated to employees and tied to specific standards and measures—your chances of getting high grades from customers for service quality are close to 90 percent.

The irreverent cartoon character Dilbert defines a vision statement as a "long, awkward sentence that demonstrates management's inability to think clearly." Make sure your own statement proves Dilbert wrong by communicating, in easily understood, jargon-free ways, the actions your people are expected to take to impress and retain customers.

A good service vision statement should have three parts:
1. It identifies your core customers.
2. It identifies your core contribution to customers.

3. It defines what you want to be famous for—in other words, your competitive distinguisher.

Consider the two service vision statements that follow.

Mall of America, Bloomington, Minnesota

Mall of America's mission provides everyone with a shared sense of purpose and direction. It defines what we do and how we work and helps us work independently as well as a team.

Our mission is as follows:

- As a *customer-focused organization*, we understand our guests' needs to make it a positive experience every time they visit.
- As a *strong business partner*, we provide marketing and excellent mall operations to support our tenants' success.
- As a *caring community partner*, we are stewards of the environment, support community endeavors, and encourage employee involvement.
- As an *outstanding business leader*, we continually enhance the reputation of the Mall of America as a successful business demonstrating professional management.
- As an *employer of choice*, we foster the growth and development of all team members within a framework of accountability, high standards, and safety, creating a great place to work.
- As a *team-based organization*, we optimize our owners' return on investment.

NuCompass Mobility, Pleasanton, California

We combine our Knowledge, Actions, Ownership, and Empathy to create an exceptional experience for people who are navigating an important life event.

- *Knowledge.* We know our clients' program, customers' needs, and our partners' roles so that we can provide our customers with informed, intelligent, and appropriate choices.

- *Actions.* We are proactive, nimble, and responsive. We work hard to do it right the first time.
- *Ownership.* We are accountable, each and every one of us, for everything we do.
- *Empathy.* We support an employee's life event. We treat it as though it were our own.

And here's a classic from one of the recognized leaders in service, the Ritz Carlton:

"We pledge to provide the finest personal service and facilities for our guests, who will always enjoy a warm, relaxed, yet refined ambience. The Ritz-Carlton experience enlivens the senses, instills well-being, and fulfills even the unexpressed wishes and needs of our guests."

Theory to Action: Creating Standards and Norms

Your work isn't over when you've crafted a compelling service vision statement. To make the vision real and actionable for your employees, the Pay Attention approach also requires concrete service *standards and norms* tied to that vision.

Service standards and norms tell customers you'll be the same reliable, responsive, and competent organization each and every time they do business with you. Most customers know enough not to expect perfection, but they do crave a consistent level of high performance. They want to know you'll provide them with the same level of customer care whether they do business on Monday morning or Friday afternoon, whether they visit your downtown location or a suburban branch, and whether they interact with call center reps, cashiers, or an anonymous face behind a computer monitor.

Standards and norms help make your service vision actionable for the workforce. Consider the last time you received performance feedback from a boss or co-worker. If that feedback was of the generic variety, as in "your attitude needs to improve," odds are it frustrated you because you didn't quite know what to do with it. Now, if your boss said, "I noticed that you haven't been using the service recovery process we've been stressing in our team meetings when you deal with unhappy customers," that would be easier to act on.

The same principle holds for service standards and norms. If management proclaims in a vision statement, "Go forth and create happy customers," but doesn't create cascading metrics and norms for what that should look like in practice, workers will be left to their own devices to define what good service means to customers.

Good service standards walk the fine line between customer expectations and internal capabilities. One example of a service standard might be: "We provide our customers with rapid response to questions or problems." A norm translates the standard into specific behaviors: "We will return all customer phone calls within two hours, respond to internal calls on the same day, respond to all customer e-mails within four hours, and respond to Twitter posts that have questions or concerns as soon as they're read."

The service vision statement at Ritz-Carlton Hotels has long stressed creating a "warm, relaxed, yet refined ambience" for guests. One way that statement is made actionable for hotel employees is with a service standard that states, "Use proper vocabulary with guests." Casual language such as "Okay" or "No problem" is replaced with "My pleasure" or "Certainly." The idea isn't to come across as stuffy or uppity but rather to match the hotel's upscale and professional setting. More recently, the hotel chain has been working hard to create flexibility and to personalize the luxury stay to the local scene. In San Francisco, for example, guests are invited to an intimate wine tasting at check-in.

It might seem like a little thing, but you'll be surprised at how the small things such as paying attention to vocabulary details can make a big difference to your customers.

Service-first companies also focus more time and energy on creating standards and norms around performance areas shown to have the biggest impact on customer loyalty. Customers of a video rental business might not care much whether a staff member greets them with a "Hello" when they enter the store, for example, but they're likely to have stronger feelings about being fairly and quickly compensated if a movie they've rented is damaged or unwatchable. The latter factor would be considered a key customer loyalty driver, and the standards and norms created around it should be handled with great care.

Hiring Tactics: Select for Attitude, Train for Skill

Paying attention to preparation also means being diligent about hiring the type of people who can execute your service strategy as devised. The best service providers we know use hiring strategies that select first for service attitude and second for job-specific skills. You can always teach a modestly intelligent person to use new technology, software, cash registers, or other service tools, the theory goes, but you can't teach them to be polite, patient, resilient, or naturally helpful. As Jim von Maur, president of Iowa-based Von Maur department stores once told us, "My dad had a theory: We can train them to sell. We can't train them to be nice; that was their parents' job."

In short, when it comes to making great service hires, what job prospects know is less important than who they are. The biggest hiring mistake we see companies make is choosing people with the right technical skills—or a history of strong performance in nonservice roles—thinking they can change their attitudes. But the old adage rings true: People don't change their spots. A large body of research shows that people's personalities, once established, don't vary much over the years.

When Netflix, the DVD rental company, eliminated its Web-based customer service and went primarily to phone-based support, it opted to locate its main call center in Hillsboro, Oregon. A driving force behind that decision was the quality of the workforce in that area, which Netflix management considered among the friendliest, most polite, and most upbeat people in the country. In other words, the available talent pool possessed a natural service orientation.

Netflix understands that an ounce of selection is worth a pound of training. If you're fanatical about choosing the right people, it follows that you should have to spend less time and fewer dollars training and managing them once they're on the job. And with fewer people doing more work as the effects of the last recession linger, Netflix also is among organizations that know that the price of making a bad hiring decision is higher than ever.

Modeling Star Performers

Attitude isn't everything, of course. Your new hires also need a strong work ethic and enough intellectual horsepower to quickly learn new technologies and work routines. One of the best ways to hire people with that full complement of skills, and to improve the odds of finding a good cultural fit, is to study service professionals in your company who are already performing at a high level. One of the earliest proponents of this strategy was Bridgeport, Pennsylvania-based consulting firm Development Dimensions International (DDI). By studying top performers and determining their key skills and attitudes, DDI found that you can develop behavior-based interview questions and role-playing scenarios that help you hire people with similar attributes.

Any good interviewing process features multiple interviews or "screens" and, more often these days, personality assessments that gauge attitude as well as job simulations that ask applicants to demonstrate how they'd handle real service situations. Although there are no "magic bullet" questions that automatically reveal an applicant's service orientation, there are some questions that work better than others. We've found these to be particularly effective in our research:

- We've all had experiences with difficult customers. Describe an example that shows how you might typically handle them?
- Let me give you a typical customer service situation we get at ABC Company (describe the scenario). How would you handle this type of situation?
- Tell me about a time when you were able to balance the best interests of the customer against the best interests of the company.
- What does giving the customer "superior service" mean to you?
- We all get tired and irritable from time to time from dealing with customers all day. How do you renew yourself so that doesn't show through to customers, so you can stay "up," fresh, and enthusiastic on the job all day?

At Southwest Airlines, the low-fare air carrier known for its distinctive customer service, those responsible for hiring service staff ask applicants to answer questions such as, "One time when my sense of humor helped me on the job was ..." and "A time I reached peak performance was ..." and more. Southwest also has been known to use a hiring exercise called Fallout Shelter, where job applicants role-play a committee charged with rebuilding civilization after a nuclear war. Applicants are given a list of 15 people from different occupations, including teacher, nurse, biochemist, pop singer, and more. They have 10 minutes to make a unanimous decision about which seven of those people should remain in the fallout shelter.

As the applicants debate and discuss, Southwest hiring managers watch their behavior, grading each on a scale ranging from *passive* to *active* to *leader;* often they look for people who are active without being domineering, or for those with poise and assertiveness. The most promising candidates are asked back for more in-depth interviews.[1]

Training and Coaching

As a service manager, it can be easy to think your job is over once people are hired and oriented to their new positions. After all, if you're doing things the right way, you've just completed an exhaustive selection process that included background checks, personality testing, multiple interviews, and role playing to ensure the right fit for the job. But your products, customer base, service policies, and business culture are unique, and if follow-up training and coaching processes aren't in place to help people learn them—and to make that training "stick"—your customers will likely be the first to know.

Companies serious about service quality invest heavily in training their people in product or service knowledge, technical skills, and dealing with upset customers. But more important than overall training dollars spent is ensuring that the training or coaching delivered is relevant and targeted to job performance. Whether it's formal classroom training, sharing of best practices over internal networks, or self-directed e-learning, the best training approaches model decisions and behaviors that employees are asked to make every day on the job.

Acknowledging how taxing it can be to interact with customers all day, more companies are also teaching customer contact personnel ways to cope with the emotional stress of their jobs—particularly stress created by abusive or overly demanding customers—and how to care for their bodies so that they can stay fresh and energized throughout long shifts of customer contact.

How important is structured training to helping your people deliver service that consistently delights customers? One study found that employees who receive formal training—the type based on sound adult learning principles and good instructional design—reach "standard" performance levels faster, create less waste, and are better at customer troubleshooting than employees who learn by the typical "sit next to John and watch how he does it" approach.[2]

The trouble with the latter method is that although John might be a star performer or subject matter expert, he too often has little experience or expertise in the art of teaching—meaning that he's not likely to instruct in ways that his co-workers learn best. Skill retention requires patient instruction, repeated, hands-on practice and corrective coaching, and often the use of clearly written job aids or "cheat sheets" to engrain new learning once the employee is back on the job.

Absent that structured approach, if trainees can't remember the commands John used with his customer contact software or how he dealt with that challenging customer question a few weeks back, their learning—and the valuable time all have invested in making it happen—will likely to go up in smoke.

Dwindling budgets and staff cutbacks, a reality during the recent recession, also have forced companies to get creative in how they train customer contact staff. Marriott Hotels, for example, cross-trained employees such as administrative assistants to help serve food at hotel banquets. Such moves helped the hotel chain keep service levels strong without adding the cost of more staff.[3]

USAA Insurance, recognized as a service leader, has taken steps to extend the learning for many of its employees. The company has initiated a program for cross-training, so that employees are better able to answer customer questions without call transfers and to fill in when call volumes fluctuate. This way the company has avoided layoffs and increased productivity.[4]

As we explored in Chapter 1, today's customers, compliments of the vast amount of data available on the Web, have more information than ever about your products and services. Thus they expect your service staff and salespeople to not only know their own products and services cold but to have a good working knowledge of the competition's offerings as well. So, the more insight and knowledge your people can provide customers, the less need customers might feel for comparison shopping. That makes ongoing training on product and service offerings, and how they are positioned against the features of competitors' product lines, a high priority for many customer call centers.

Because of this priority, the following are several questions to ask so that you ensure your product and service training exceeds the customer's knowledge base:

- What do your products or services do?
- What is it that they can't do (or aren't doing)?
- What is it that your competitors' products and services can and cannot do?
- What is your unique selling proposition (and that of your competition)?
- How does each product or service benefit a customer?
- How have customers used your product or service (and your competition's product or service) to improve their business?
- What are the trends in the industry that can or will impact your sales and customer perceptions?

When each employee can answer these questions, you are truly adding value for your customers. This type of training exceeds customer expectations and will perhaps deter customers from visiting your competition and making a comparison. Couple this with thorough listening to match the customer's needs, wants, and expectations to the very best product to meet those needs, and your company will be a force to be reckoned with.

And though it's standard for companies to provide their employees with a list of questions that customers most frequently ask about their products and services, the best service providers also usually provide a list of common complaints about their offerings, as well as the competition's, so that front-line staff is well prepared to respond.

Internal Social Networks: Cost-Effective Learning Tools

All this advice about continual training sounds good in theory, but the reality of the working world means that it's not always easy to find the time or budget to train your people. With the downsizing that's accompanied the recent economic downturn, employees are often doing the work of their departed colleagues, and because of that bigger workload they usually have little time for additional skills training. Training budgets, long a target for cuts when company revenues suffer, also have been squeezed tighter than ever.

That reality requires that you get more resourceful at finding ways to deliver cost-effective training in shorter bursts. One way some are doing that is by creating internal social networks designed to help employees share best practices and organizational know-how. At Best Buy Co., the electronics superstore, an internal network called Blue Shirt Nation enables employees to easily share knowledge, best practices, and even frustrations they experience in working with customers. More than 20,000 Best Buy employees regularly use this online "swap meet" to exchange ideas about how best to service customers, discuss sales approaches that worked (or fell flat), get updates on new technologies, and more. In one case, a Best Buy executive posted to the site an idea about changing an employee discount policy. The post was met with a flurry of negative comments from Best Buy employees, which led managers to reexamine the idea and eventually decide against any changes.

IBM Corp. views internal social networks as a just-in-time learning tool that can help narrow the gap between learning and application. Using IBM's vast internal network, employees often have online discussions around serving clients and can search for one another based on experience in a particular industry or with particular clients. Proposals are swapped and hard-won lessons about serving customers are shared. The network also enables users to easily locate IBM subject matter experts and send questions via instant messages or e-mail for informal coaching.[5]

Another cost-effective learning tool is the self-assessment. Done right, this approach gives your people a mirror in which to view their current performance levels. You can, for example, encourage employees who deal with customers on the phone to record several phone conversations and evaluate them alone or with the help of an experienced peer. Or consider videotaping role playing in service training sessions as a way to get people to see how others perceive them.

Pay Attention to What's Rewarded and Measured

How you measure the performance of customer contact staff, and how you compensate or recognize them for what they do in the name of service excellence, also sends a powerful message about what's important to the organization—and what your people should pay attention to.

In making its daring switch from e-mail to phone-based customer support, Netflix managed to avoid one trap that many organizations fall into. Rather than implementing measures of customer service performance that were primarily efficiency or productivity based—for example, average handle time, length of customer call, and so on—the company focused more on measuring call center representatives on factors tied to issue resolution, call quality, and customer service metrics.

Netflix wants its service people to ensure that customers hang up the phone knowing their issues have been resolved or their complaints have had a fair hearing, rather than feeling gently forced off the phone or cut short so that reps can meet their length-of-call numbers. In the end, Netflix management understands that the customer loyalty gained from such an approach—and the resulting revenue realized from repeat business—outweighs any cost savings the company might gain from reducing phone expenses.

Zappos.com, the online shoe seller, is another company that does little monitoring of its service representatives' call times and provides them no scripts for handling customer conversations. Such conditions, designed to put customer satisfaction ahead of efficiency metrics, require a special breed of empowered employee. To guarantee a good cultural fit, the company's CEO has offered new customer service agents up to $2,000 to leave the company after an initial training period if they don't think they're cut out for the job. As of this writing fewer than 10 percent have taken him up on the offer.

At the management level, organizations such as T-Mobile pay executive bonuses only if managers pass Retail Certification—working a week in the retail store plus an extra day during the holidays. This practice gives execs instant credibility when they do visit a store. Or, at Enterprise Rent-a-Car, agency managers say they're in ESQI jail, which stands for the Enterprise Service Quality Index, and won't be promoted if their scores fall below average.[6] Every level and department of an organization needs to be enveloped in the service effort and reward structure.

Companies that take the Pay Attention strategy to heart also strive to treat their service employees in the same way they treat VIP customers, and that starts with providing competitive pay and benefits. At Ultimate Software, the Weston, Florida-based provider of human resources software solutions, CEO Scott Scherr turns the typical corporate totem pole on its head. Employees are clearly number one, followed by customers and then shareholders.

Besides ample health care coverage, every employee receives stock options and a 30 percent company match to their 401K plans. Since founding the company 20 years ago, Scherr hasn't laid off any employees, despite enduring some rocky times, and Ultimate has consistently made lists of the top medium-sized companies to work for in the United States.

Only by treating employees right does Scherr believe they can deliver the type of customer service that consistently wins—and retains—clients. In 2008 Ultimate had a customer retention rate of 97 percent, a number also influenced by the user-friendliness and utility of the firm's software applications. Ultimate believes that employees who feel respected and honored by their bosses are more motivated and productive and more apt to go above and beyond to satisfy customers. Consider the actions taken by one Ultimate service representative a few years ago. The rep received a call in the wee hours from a panicked customer of First Horizon National Bank who was experiencing a vexing problem with some payroll software. The Ultimate rep stayed on the phone with the customer until 2:00 A.M. to fix the problem and provided her home number in case the client needed additional help.[7]

If you're seeking more of a certain kind of service behavior, it's also important to remember the adage "Catch somebody doing something right today." In the constant rush of serving customers, doing paperwork, or troubleshooting problems, it can be easy for managers to forget to recognize or celebrate their people for the good service they provide to customers every day. But nothing is more important to sustaining a Pay Attention strategy than regular encouragement for your hardworking service staff.

Plenty of research shows that many high-performing service employees leave their jobs not because they think their salaries or benefits are too low but because they feel unappreciated by their bosses. Whether it's a formal award for a "beyond the call of duty" service act, a simple "thank you" or handwritten note for a job well done, or treating your service team to lunch in appreciation for doing the hard emotional labor of serving customers all day, such acts of recognition make a lasting impact on the recipients.

In short, it's easy to lose sight of how powerful a sincere "You did a great job, thanks" is to keeping the Pay Attention spirit alive and well in your organization.

Chapter 4

PAY ATTENTION TO THE CUSTOMER EXPERIENCE

E very customer is unique. Whether it's a dining experience, shopping for the latest fashions, or surfing the Web for a great last-minute getaway, each customer has her own expectations of how the experience should play out. In a Pay Attention focus, the goal is to make the experience personal and memorable for each customer.

Consider this example told to us by a seatmate on an airline flight. Needing to take his car in for service, Pete scheduled an appointment with the dealership where he always had his car repaired. His engine light had recently come on and he needed to get it checked out. On arrival, his service agent greeted him warmly by name. As Pete explained his repair needs, the agent carefully made notes, asked relevant questions, and confirmed what he heard. After the agent provided an estimate of how long the repair might take, our new acquaintance set off to work in the van provided by the dealership. Later that day the dealership called Pete. The ensuing conversation delighted the car owner. He learned that the pesky "service engine soon" light had to do with a gas cap that had lost its ability to close tightly and was losing pressure. The fix was not only easy, it was inexpensive. But what made this a positive memorable experience was that the dealership topped off his engine fluids, filled his gas tank to test the new gas cap, and washed his car—at no additional charge. Upon picking up his car, Pete found a reminder sheet of the upcoming warranty-recommended service and a prioritized list of how to schedule the work. Wow!

Contrast this to a similar car repair experience Jill had. Her "service engine soon" light also came on, and she went to her favorite dealership to see what the issue was. After hooking the car up to the computer—the only way for the mechanic to identify the problem—she learned that it was going to cost her $102 just to be told that she had neglected to tighten her gas cap the last time she filled her tank, and that was just the car's way of letting her know. She was not a happy customer, even though she received most of the same perks that Pete received. The clean car and topped-off fluids were nice, but they didn't make up for the $102 she had to cough up due to her own negligence.

Here we have two very similar stories that left two very different impressions on customers. The value-added service provided in both cases was exemplary, but only one customer went away happy. The lesson here is that what is important to one person might not be important to another. Each customer is unique, and determining the different ways they define service quality requires rapt attention and relentless listening.

Make It Personal

Service masters have an obsession with their customers. They listen to them, study them, and learn from them. They are constantly trying to crawl inside their heads to find out what makes them tick. However, these masters do not simply take orders from their customers. Rather, they synthesize their sense of customers' wants, needs, and expectations into unique, clever, and sometimes highly innovative personal solutions.

Take Charles Schwab, the investment services firm. The company was hearing from customers that they didn't like to deal with the company's automated phone line when they had to call Schwab a second time to deal with a question or problem. So the company created a simple new direct-dial feature that lets repeat clients call a Schwab representative directly to resolve an issue, rather than have to again slash through the underbrush of an automated phone system to get what they want.

The company also created a "flex force" service team designed to jump on phone lines in times of high calling demand, such as when the market takes a sharp decline.[1] Both improvements were a result of listening closely to customers for their "pain points" and moving quickly to staunch the bleeding.

JetBlue Airways also understands the importance of value-added, personalized service. The low-cost airline offers a first checked bag free of charge as well as a live in-flight entertainment system with 36 channels of free DirectTV, 100 channels of free radio, and unlimited complimentary in-flight snacks. Customers can enjoy the entertainment in JetBlue's roomy seats, which allow the kind of legroom in coach that's difficult to find on any other U.S. airline. JetBlue is clearly a business that keeps the customer experience top of mind, evidenced by it being named by J. D. Power and Associates, a global market research company, as tops in airline customer satisfaction among low-cost carriers in 2009. It was the fourth year in a row that the company captured the award.

Whether your customer comes to you via the Internet, the front door, or the telephone, there is gold to mine in the knowledge gained from these interactions. Certainly there are computer systems and software that gather data and offer myriad options for reviewing, analyzing, and applying the data. But not every organization can afford such systems. What all companies do have are human beings that talk to, e-mail, tweet, or face the customer every day. In some ways this is the best system of all: employees having daily conversations with customers across channels to find out what pleases them about how you conduct business, what improvements they might suggest to your operations, and what makes them want to pull out their hair about the way they're treated or the hoops they're made to jump through.

You'll find that companies with some of the best service reputations welcome and even embrace negative feedback. Although they won't make changes based on all of it, nor will they consider all rants or suggested changes realistic or relevant, they know that only by hearing directly from the customer can they identify weak spots in service delivery that drive people away, often under the company's radar.

Each interaction with a customer provides an opportunity to Pay Attention and learn what's important to that individual. From that vantage point, the service provider may customize the outcome to make it unique to that customer. Now, repeated many times over, it might not feel unique to the service associate, but it should always feel unique and personal to the customer. What is available to help make it so? Well, start with the customer's name. How about buying history? What is evident about the nature of the interaction? Perhaps a sense of urgency? What small, low-cost touches can you add that will make each experience memorable? If customers are repeat visitors, can you do something special to acknowledge their return? When service providers are trained to really know their products and services, they are freed up to focus on improving the customer experience.

Consider web sites that personalize the individual online experience when you log in. On Amazon.com, your prior purchase history allows that site to make recommendations of new items that might interest you. When you look up a book or music title, Amazon shows you what others who have looked at those same titles not only reviewed but purchased. At Netflix, customers are provided lists of movies similar in content or style to those they've already rented, a service that's proven highly popular. When you log onto an airline web site, it might show you your upcoming travel plans as well as the latest deals on frequently traveled destinations or perhaps your mileage reward level and current award status. As customers, when we see this personalized information, it makes us feel valued and appreciated—special to that company.

Customer-facing employees have access to vast numbers of customers across multiple touch points, and service-savvy organizations are finding ways to allow them to do the work they do best: connect with and listen to customers. In larger organizations, dedicated service teams are trolling the Web with tracking software such as Radian6 to find out what individuals are saying about their organizations, with the goal of gathering feedback and solving problems so that they can enhance the customer experience.

In smaller organizations with more limited resources, employees are carving out parts of workdays to monitor customer feedback on review sites such as Yelp or comments left on their own web sites, or to alert devoted customers to product deals or coupons by way of their Facebook pages or Twitter accounts.

Corporate web sites offer a great place to build communities. Community simply means that a site is more than a place to buy, it's a place to learn, share, and communicate with others. It allows visitors to make the site their own by joining a conversation or learning new facts. People have always expected to find communities online, and they search for them. If you've got a product that excites people, give them a chance to share their excitement.

One organization, Norwegian Cruise Lines (NCL), discovered that its travelers loved to tell stories of their travel experiences and share reviews and opinions. The cruise line became one of the first to create its own online community forum, called *Freestyle Voices* (www.ncl.com/FreestyleVoices). Since its short time online the site has captured 770 shore reviews, 200 posted stories, and some 3,500 submitted questions. The forum allows NCL to gather critical data about and from its customers; better tailor service options to the individual; and suggest links to other areas of the NCL site.

NCL also knows that one advantage of creating such forums is that more customers are drawn to its web site, and not to the blogosphere or social media at large, to discuss their experiences with the organization. That gives it a better chance to identify and address any problems internally before customers might opt to take them to, say, Twitter, Facebook, or YouTube and potentially do harm to the company's reputation.

Adding community is actually a fairly cheap addition to any web site because visitors create the bulk of the content. One payoff is that visitors feel like the site is a place they'd want to visit again because it appeals to part of the psyche. It gives them a sense that you care about their interests and that you built your site with them in mind. A place that lets the customer link with peers is far more worthy of a bookmark than a strictly e-commerce site, regardless of how attractively it's built. Another huge payoff is that control piece. You have the ability to address problems, questions, or misinformation quickly and cleanly.

Whatever strategy you choose, strive to make sure the customer experience is unique and personal. Customers repeatedly tell us how wonderful it is to feel special, and you don't need to break the bank to create that feeling. Sometimes all it takes is using a customer's name, taking a little extra time to let the customer vent, or sending a short follow-up note thanking them for their business. Remember that the fewer human contacts people have with your organization, the more important each one becomes. Not only that, but people tell us over and over again that a personalized service experience plays a significant role in their repurchase intentions. Organizations today need to do everything they can to get an upper hand on the competition, and making service personal goes a long way toward achieving that objective.

Social Media Plays a Role at Comcast

One of industries most vilified for poor customer service is cable television. It's long been the target of customer derision and jokes about service outages, phone calls that go unreturned, and repairmen who show up late or not at all. One infamous YouTube video shows a Comcast technician dozing on a customer's couch, having fallen asleep while on hold on the phone with his own office.

But since 2008 Comcast Corp. has been working feverishly to change that image with its comprehensive new Customer Care program. The makeover is designed to create a renewed service focus in a culture that long seemed to put customer concerns on the back burner. The trick will be whether Comcast executives are still talking about and applying resources toward customer service issues three or four years down the road. Only then will we know whether a service-first culture is taking root.

One part of the service initiative is focused on listening to Comcast customers and addressing their concerns via social media channels such as Twitter. Frank Eliason, Comcast's senior director, National Customer Service, had the idea of using Twitter to engage Comcast customers with questions or concerns about the service. By doing a search for the word Comcast—or far less flattering nicknames for the organization—he discovered that he could find Twitter users who were talking about service issues he could address.

By the end of 2008, the organization had handled some 20,000 tweets that addressed customer service concerns.

Comcast doesn't view social media as a replacement for traditional service channels such as 800 numbers or e-mail but rather as a complement that offers a more informal, immediate way to address customer issues. Twitter is sometimes used to follow up with customers who haven't had their needs met through other service avenues. Instead of having to endure a maddening wait on a phone call customers can have their complaints acknowledged immediately via a tweet.

In one example, a tweet from a Comcast customer mentioned that he was having problems with the company's Internet service. In responding, Eliason hit Twitter's direct message (DM) button, which allowed him to communicate privately with the customer via e-mail, whereupon Eliason asked for the customer's phone number. Employing a user interface tool, Eliason could check to see whether the customer's modem was functioning properly and had the problem fixed in short order.[2]

In another case Eliason engaged a customer on Twitter who tweeted after experiencing a service failure trifecta: His cable, phone, and Internet service all went out following a visit from a Comcast serviceperson. Eliason searched the Comcast database for the customer's cell phone number, called him directly, and offered help. He was able to determine that the problem was outside the customer's house and arranged for a technician to arrive post-haste to make the needed changes.

Over time Eliason opted to replace the Comcast corporate logo that accompanied his tweets with his own photo, a move designed to add a more human touch to his advice on Twitter. That helped users think of him more as "Frank," and as a result he created thousands of followers who now follow his tweets and even know about his family web site.

Taking Problems Seriously

The Twitter tactics are just one part of Comcast's new customer service makeover. The Customer Care program also includes giving service technicians handheld devices that can test a home's entire network, expanding technicians' hours to Sundays and handing out "Make It Right" cards to any customers who experience a problem with their cable service; the cards include a special phone number to call.

Comcast wants its employees to hand out the cards when they encounter anyone who complains in any fashion about the cable provider, from neighbors talking over a back fence to fans at a sporting event or people at a happy-hour gathering. The cards promise priority assistance to anyone calling the special number.

Although it's taken some time, Comcast has come to realize that the service basics matter more than anything to customers. That includes enabling customers to easily reach someone on Twitter or over the phone to get problems fixed quickly and competently, teaching call-center reps to listen more effectively and be respectful, and having service techs simply show up at the time promised.

The revamped efforts appear to be paying early dividends. According to the American Customer Satisfaction Index, which tracks consumer opinions of hundreds of companies, Comcast's score rose 9 percent in 2009—not a quantum leap but a move in the right direction. You can check out Comcast Cares at http://twitter.com/comcastcares.[3]

Be ETDBW: Easy to Do Business With

Although we all love to be treated like snowflakes—as one of a kind, never to walk the earth again—the reality is that we share many of the same service needs. And one of those is a desire to transact business with organizations in the most convenient and hassle-free ways possible.

The more times we have to call a company back to resolve a frustrating problem, the more times we walk the aisles of a store without receiving a sniff of assistance, or the more times we endlessly search a poorly designed web site for information, the greater the odds we'll start looking for someplace else to spend our money. More than ever, today's busy customers value and fastidiously protect their time. The easier and more convenient you can make it to do business with you—given that you're also providing quality products at competitive prices—the better the chance you'll turn people into loyal, longtime customers.

Although this might seem an obvious point, it's one that's apparently overlooked or downplayed by many organizations. A few years ago, we developed an inventory of characteristics and practices that distinguish between organizations that delight and retain their customers and those that marginally satisfy and frequently lose customers. The survey differentiated companies that focused on transactions from those that created value for and long-term relationships with their customers. One statistically significant factor is the ETDBW aptitude: being "easy to do business with."

Paying Attention to the customer experience means that you are focused on making it so easy for customers to do business with you that they'll have little reason to look for greener pastures and will enthusiastically recommend you to others.

ETDBW organizations make it easy for customers to obtain their products, information, or services—on their own terms—just as they make it easy for customers to reach the right individual, area, or resolution system when they have a problem or question.

Consider for a moment how frustrating it is when you dial a company's 800 number—particularly if you've just searched exhaustively for it on a web site, only to find it tucked away in microscopic print under a nonintuitive category—and then only to be greeted with an automated phone menu. Although the recorded voice might be friendly and constantly remind you that "you're a valued customer," you wait patiently without hearing the option you believe best meets your needs. Because you're limited to only the options offered, in frustration you select one that you think is close enough.

When you're asked to enter your account number to best direct your call, you do so. Once you're transferred, if you're lucky enough to reach a human being, you're asked to provide the 16-digit account number yet again. By this point you'd be forgiven for pounding the phone against a wall. Such systems are the antithesis of being easy to do business with. They are designed from the inside looking out rather than the outside looking in. In other words, they're built primarily to reduce operating costs, with little consideration for the customer experience.

What does an ETDBW service delivery system look like in action? From the customer's point of view, the "customer-friendliest" delivery systems are as follows:

- *Accessible.* You can reach the company easily and in multiple ways. Where are your customers likely to look for you? Your web site? Twitter or other social media? E-mail? Employ as many options as you can manage.
- *Accurate.* Regardless of the topic, all the information that's accessible to customers must be accurate. If it's not, customers will see right through the inaccuracies and not return for more abuse.
- *Integrated.* Customers can get all the information they need from one source. And your sources—web site, 800 number, tweets, blogs, bricks-and-mortar, customer service representatives (CSRs), online chat options—need to be perceived as seamless to the customer. Regardless of the way a customer chooses to engage your organization, the channels must be open, easy, consistent, and knowledgeable.
- *Customer-driven.* The customer can understand and use the information, systems, and options without hoops to jump through. In addition, all forms of engagement should offer the customer what he wants, when he wants it.
- *Fast.* In this time of instant communication, customers are less willing to wait than ever before for answers to questions or resolutions to problems. The speed at which information travels is critical to your success. Immediacy is what's made channels like Twitter such a valuable way to address customer concerns. Customers can alert companies to problems via tweets, and service staff can follow up through other channels such as phone or e-mail if needed.
- *Totally transparent.* If there are details that need to be handled, they should be outside the customer's field of vision or so well integrated that the customer doesn't even know they happen. Think of a duck swimming upstream. What you see

above the water line is a calm quacker. Below the water, the poor duck is paddling like crazy!

EDTBW considerations are different between bricks-and-mortar companies and those that do business online. Consider the new restaurant that opens in the heart of a major business district. Regardless of the quality of the food, the attitude of the wait staff, or the price, the restaurant is likely to do decent business simply because of the proximity to the market. But in the world of e-commerce, customers don't notice you as they walk down the street; they have to seek you out. They won't return out of convenience or because you're located just around the block from their home, since they can just as easily go to a hundred other sites with the same ease as visiting yours. With the increase in online shopping, it's more important than ever that you be easy to do business with.

Consider the changes that the Artful Home, a retailer that sells artists' original works, made to its web site in the name of being ETDBW. Research found that visitors to the site often had difficulty locating what they were after; some 30 percent of searches to the site produced no results. One problem was the way customers spelled words in searches. For example, because some people have a hard time spelling *jewelry*, their searches on the site would produce the result, "Sorry, we don't have any *<misspelled word>*," which in regards to jewelry was far from the case. So, as part of its web site redesign, the Artful Home employed a new search tool that provides results for commonly misspelled words.

Other site design changes streamlined content and made navigation easier for customers. In the previous design, for example, there were 20-plus categories listed on the left-hand navigation column; the redesign now features the five best-selling categories run across the top of the page. Product images also were made about 200 percent larger, for easier viewing by customers.

The company quickly saw positive results from the design changes. After the redesign went live in 2007, sales from online marketing efforts increased 153 percent, and customer searches producing no results dropped from 30 percent to 8 percent.[4]

Being ETDBW Means Considering All Audiences

You need to buy a wedding gift, and you know the happy couple is registered at a variety of stores. Opting to pull up their registries online, you decide to make a purchase at one of the web sites. But here's the rub: When you click on the product's full details, you see that what you want to purchase cannot be returned to the store. It has to be shipped back to the address designated on the packing slip.

Purchasing the wedding gift may be easy for you, the buyer. But what about the recipient? Organizations must consider being ETDBW for ultimate end users as well as purchasers. There also may be a restocking charge that isn't listed prominently on the site. Is this an ETDBW, customer-friendly way to do business? It's a question it pays to ask for any process or procedure that affects customers of any stripe.

Catching on to these concerns, Target, the Minneapolis-based retail store chain, now makes most of the items purchased on its web site available for return at a local store. Now that's keeping ETDBW top of mind.

Organizations keen on customer retention also regularly review their policies and procedures to ensure they're not sending the wrong message to customers and that they assist rather than constrain associates in delivering excellent service and quickly solving customer problems.

Front-line associates in organizations committed to being ETDBW are often empowered to act on behalf of the customer while maintaining the best interests of the organization. They know their limits and boundaries, and because of careful training, they often don't need authorization for daily decisions, meaning they can avoid putting customers through the frustrating "I'll need to consult my supervisor about this" delays that usually

involve call transfers and waits on hold. The rules of engagement are grounded in customer expectations and contribute to
meeting customer needs, making associates humane, not robotic.

Payoffs of Being ETDBW

Paying Attention to the customer experience isn't simply a nice
thing to do for customers, it also has bottom-line payoffs. Combine quality products or services with an ETDBW service culture
and you have a value package that's hard to beat—and one likely
to boost your customer retention rates.

And one thing we know for sure is that keeping the customers
you have is a whole lot cheaper than continually trying to refill
the cupboards with new ones. In fact, according to research from
Boston-based Bain and Co., it will cost you five to seven times more
to obtain a new customer than to keep the customer you already
have, owing largely to the high costs of advertising or marketing
that's needed to convince new customers to try your offerings.

Smart business leaders see the value of customers beyond a
single transaction. For example, while the dollar value of a customer's one-time oil change might be $21.95, projected over 10
to 15 years, that customer— should she remain loyal—will bring
her car in every three to four months and is worth thousands of
dollars to the organization, particularly if she's also buying add-
on services for her car. No need for any additional advertising
or marketing expenditures to keep this customer on board—just
continue to meet or exceed her product or service expectations
and her money will continue to fall to your bottom line.

Remember, too, that this customer loyalty calculation doesn't
take into account any word-of-mouth benefits you receive from
that customer referring your business to others, which she is likely
to do if you treat her right.

When you look at each customer this way, as an asset worth
thousands or even millions of dollars over a lifetime, your
viewpoint naturally shifts from one of customer acquisition to one
of customer retention. Figure 4.1 demonstrates a way to make this

calculation and moves on to include the life of that customer's continued business (Compound Value) and the impact of losing this customer and those she tells if she has a bad experience (Potential Impact).

Equation 1

SIMPLE VALUE OF A (LOST) CUSTOMER

Value of an average service transaction   (a)   _____

Times the average number of transactions per   (b)   × _____
customer each year

Simple (loss) value for that customer   (c)   ═══════

Equation 2

COMPOUND VALUE OF A (LOST) CUSTOMER

Times average life of a customer (number of   (d)   × _____
years a customer is likely to do business with
you)

Compound value of a (lost) customer   (e)   ═══════

Equation 3

POTENTIAL IMPACT OF A LOST CUSTOMER

Times the average number of people the
customer will tell about his or her
disappointment. If you don't know for your
industry, use eight (your original customer
plus seven other people who are influenced)   (f)   × _____

Potential impact of a lost customer   (g)   ═══════

Figure 4.1 Value of a Lost Customer

Responsiveness and Reliability: Keys to the Customer Experience

Two of the biggest influences on customer loyalty are responsiveness and reliability, factors found among the all-important

RATER dimensions we detailed in Chapter 1. Responsiveness is the willingness to help and provide prompt, competent service upon a customer's first contact with your company. Regardless of which service channel or department is the point of contact for customers, it's the responsibility of all involved individuals to Pay Attention to the customer experience.

In a 2008 survey conducted by Convergys, the U.S. Customer Scorecard, 64 percent of respondents said that addressing customer needs on first contact is a key service differentiator. The more times a customer has to repeat a story, provide an account number, or call back to ask the same question, the more frustrated he becomes—and the more prone to defection. Conversely, solve the customer's problem or answer a question in one friendly and efficient phone call, Twitter interaction, or e-mail—with no transfers, long waits on hold, or need for callbacks—and satisfaction rises substantially.

Responsiveness is also about the follow-up and follow-through you provide. Being proactive in alerting a customer to a short shipment, a delay in delivery, or a repair technician who'll be an hour late helps you manage that customer's emotional response. Treating each customer as a valued asset will make it easier, although not always more pleasant, to deliver news she might not want to hear.

Reliability—the ability to provide what was promised, dependably and accurately—is also crucial to the customer experience. When a customer is comfortable with you and your organization, it makes it easy for that customer to return, over and over again. When customers know what to expect each and every time they do business with your organization, it reinforces consistency and predictability. If the message is "You're valued and special to our organization" each time the customer interacts with you, they trust that the next visit will likely be the same. If you keep your promises time and time again, trust begins to compound. That's important, because reliability is all about reducing surprises or variations of the negative sort.

Consider the retail giant Target. If you have a Target store in your area, you likely know where we're headed with this. When Ann took her daughter to college, she had some requests for additional items for her dorm room. Having passed a Target on the way into the new college community, her daughter asked Ann if they could shop there. On entering the store, her daughter commented, "It feels like home." The look, signage, and product mix were similar to those at her local store. It was a comfortable, reliable touchstone in a new environment far away from home. That's the kind of consistency and reliability that builds loyalty.

Even Service Icons Can Fail to Pay Attention

Walt Disney World has long been known as an exemplar of reliability, or delivering a consistently high level of service quality, day in and out. Customers know that if they're dealing with the mighty Mouse, they're apt to receive the ultimate in care. But sometimes even the best of the best falter when they fail to pay close attention to parts of their operations that touch customers.

Booking a trip to Disney World would, on the surface, seem pretty straightforward. Call your travel agent or hop online, make your air reservations, get a hotel, and you're on your way. However, savvy Disney travelers have learned that is just scratching the surface. Disney guests must decide whether they're going to stay off-site or on-site, what kind of tickets they're going to purchase, if they're going to purchase one of the three food plans that Disney offers, and perhaps most important, what kind of shoes will prevent the most blisters. Enter Disboards.com.

Disboards.com is not a Disney-run site. It does, however, have several Disney cast members who respond to questions and queries on their own.

(continued)

(*Continued*)

In October 2009 Disney World upgraded its Advanced Dinner Reservation (ADR) system. Previously, guests were able to make dinner reservations 90 days in advance of their visit. Under the new system, reservations would be allowed to be made 180 days prior to visiting. This change brought with it considerable chaos. Adding to the confusion, in March 2009 Disney had just changed the system from 180 to 90 days—and less than a year later the process was being reversed.

On the morning of the system debut, diehard Disboard.com fans were wide awake and phoning into the call center by 6:00 A.M. central time, hoping to secure their coveted breakfast with Cinderella in her castle. Many were still attempting to reach a Disney cast member more than six hours later and were not overly impressed with the new system. System glitches (reservations may now also be made online), unending "All circuits are busy" messages, and long hold times once callers did get through all led to significant frustration. Keep in mind that Disney's call center is not a toll-free number; waiting callers were paying significant long distance charges without getting assistance. Even more unsettling was the fact that, if guests would call back with the same question more than once, they would sometimes get a different response from a different cast member. Again, the performance fell well short of Disney's typical reliability standards.

More than 1,500 replies and 54,000 views were posted within the first 24 hours of the launch of the new system in a thread titled "October 27, 2009, 180 Day Reservation Thread." Below is a sampling of those comments:

- Not feeling "the love" for the happiest place on earth! Been redialing for 1 hr 20 mins now and still just getting the busy signal!

- I finally got through, no wait time, but the CM I got had her computer crash, so she transferred me to someone who had a working computer. Then when she transferred me I got cut off! NOOOOOOOOOOOOOOOOOOO!
- Uggh ... Why did Disney change the old system??? I thought it was working just fine!!! Seriously!
- After 1 hour of internet failure and 1 hour of auto re-dialing ... and then 30 minutes of holding ... I JUST SPENT AN HOURRRRRR setting everything up and their system crashed. They lost allllllllllll of my reservations before they could actually book them. Their resolution ... call back in 3 hours and see if it's back up. I am sooooo angry. He said their system is seriously crashing right now.
- I called at 7:03 this morning and got through on the first try—no wait. Made ressies for Chef Mickey's and Akershus but CRT wasn't loaded yet. Man, I can't believe how lucky I was! I'd say just keep trying!
- I'm just wondering why they continue to open the phone lines if the system is unable to book any dining reservations. It does seem like some people are getting CMs who can book while others are getting ones who say they can't. Does it depend on the ability of the CM? Does it depend on the location of the different call centers?

As you can see, there is a wide range of customer feedback. Many customers are frustrated, some are encouraging, but here's the key: These are Disney's prime customers. They are diehard, loyal Mouseketeers. What impression would this situation have left on someone who's never been to one of Disney's theme parks and who might not have viewed the

(*continued*)

(*Continued*)

shoddy service as an exception to the rule? How much revenue did Disney World potentially lose by not having a reliable system in place or cast members who are thoroughly and consistently trained in the new system?

From all the posts we've read, Disney has done nothing to try to compensate customers who experienced long waits or were unable to make reservations because of system or training breakdowns.

You're only as good as your last service performance, and in this case Disney's renowned customer care left plenty to be desired.

Comments were found at http://disboards.com/showthread .php?t=2317106.

Paying attention to the customer experience pays off in dividends, both immediately and over time. Tuning in to customers' perspectives to make their experience the very best it can be creates positive, memorable first impressions. Creating opportunities for customers to make connections and want to come back builds their social capital and investment in your organization. Customer engagement, investment, and ultimately referral are the true test of loyalty.

Chapter 5

PAY ATTENTION TO NEW FEEDBACK CHANNELS

Customers want their voices to be heard. That's always been the case, but what's new is the vast number of outlets they have at their disposal to make their opinions known. Do you recall the hard-copy surveys that would arrive in the mail that you'd fill out and return to vendors to evaluate a service experience or new product purchase? We didn't think so, since it's likely been eons since you've received one. Today's customers aren't keen on engaging in such a seemingly cumbersome feedback process, nor are they willing to wait a couple of weeks or months to receive a survey. No, most want to make their voices heard, and heard *now*. And they have plenty of new avenues for making that happen.

The question is, are you willing to travel to the online communities where they're gathering and then listen to the candid feedback they're providing?

Many organizations are hooked on collecting data—all kinds of information that answers those "How am I doing?" questions—that can be used to either confirm or correct performance. This feedback comes in many forms and from a variety of sources. We track customer calls handled per hour or day, on-time deliveries against standard, customers per register, and more. Such feedback can be addictive. We love to know how we did compared to yesterday, this month compared to last, in our department versus a group in another building, or against the people on another shift.

But amid that fervor to compile and compare data, are we really listening to what customers are telling us across these new channels, or are we simply going through the motions to ease our conscience about "letting customers be heard"? It's one thing to listen to and capture the voice of the customer; it's quite another to analyze and apply that feedback in ways that enhance the customer experience.

Eleven Ways to Listen to Customers

Of course you can't act on customer feedback until you've gathered it, and you can't be a fly on the wall until you know exactly where customers are gathering "virtually," or online, to talk or blog about your business. Here are 11 of the most common methods today's customers use to tell you how they're feeling about your organization and the products and services you provide:

1. *Customer surveys.* Face-to-face, via e-mail, on web sites, or over the telephone (or through a combination of these contact methods), ask customers to rate you on overall satisfaction or "delight," on the success of the last transaction they had with you, on specific aspects of your service delivery system, and perhaps most important, on how likely they'd be to recommend you to colleagues or friends. The latter question measures how well you've done at creating "passionate promoters" of your company.
2. *Toll-free hotlines.* A good service recovery system almost always has a phone hotline of some sort, with service employees trained and focused on resolving customer problems

on first contact. Many customer-centric companies create 800-number lines for specific product or service offerings, and others have gone multilingual; FedEx, for example, has an interactive voice response system that allows customers to speak to either English or Spanish customer service personnel. Customers who call in to register a complaint, make a suggestion, ask a question, or have a problem solved offer extremely valuable input on your service delivery system.

3. *E-mail.* Many customers still rely on e-mail as a way to communicate their pleasure or displeasure with their service experience or simply to ask questions. As a private form of communication, e-mail offers an opportunity for you to respond to and resolve customer issues before they potentially go public to a wider online audience.

4. *Your own company web site.* Managing customer relationships and experiences on your turf is much preferred and more controllable then having customers go elsewhere to give feedback. Whenever possible, you should strive to be the master of your own domain by actively soliciting customer feedback and reviews of your products and services (where it makes sense) on your own web site. This requires an individual or team of people dedicated to ensuring that customer queries, orders, concerns, complaints, and praise are responded to in a timely, efficient, and warm and friendly manner. Give your customers a reason to come back to your site and leave their feedback; make it a win/win for both of you.

5. *Industry-specific review web sites.* TripAdvisor.com, Vehix.com, Steves-Digicams.com, and countless others are examples of industry-specific review sites. These sites offer consumers an opportunity to review a product or service in specific industries, such as hotel quality on TripAdvisor, and are helpful to other potential buyers. Some of the sites allow interaction with businesses; some do not. Some allow you to contact the reviewer; some do not. However, knowing

what's being said about your product or service can enable you to make changes where warranted. If 90 percent of reviewers are indicating that the battery life of your newest camera release is too short and not worth the extra money, that gives you input into changes that might need to be made in product development. On the other hand, if only 1 percent of customers review your hotel and describe the front desk as rude, unfriendly, and unhelpful, you have to respond differently to that smaller sample of negative feedback.

6. *Facebook.* With more than 400 million active users as of this writing, Facebook sees more than 50 percent of its users log onto the site on any given day. Perhaps surprisingly, Facebook's fastest-growing user demographic consists of people older than 35 years of age. An astounding 8 billion minutes are spent on Facebook each day worldwide, and there are more than 45 million daily status updates.

   With numbers like that, can your organization afford to not be a part of this current phenomenon? Your customers are out there! More and more businesses are relying on Facebook "fan" pages to build loyalty, connect to customers, send out marketing appeals, and promote new products. Recently, the TGI Friday's restaurant chain introduced Woody, who had the job of trying to attract 500,000 fans to Friday's Facebook page. Once the goal was reached, all fans received a coupon for a free Jack Daniels Burger. To date, Woody has more than 977,000 fans—which translates to nearly a million prospective TGI Friday's customers who are aware of what Friday's is up to . . . via Woody, of course. The possibilities for organizations are endless! Your customers are looking for you—and they're talking. Each one has, on average, 130 friends! Are you taking advantage of that opportunity? Should you be?

7. *YouTube.* Did you know that YouTube.com is now the number-two search engine? That's right; it's second only

to Google. YouTube is no longer used just for viewing last night's reality TV result or the latest celebrity *faux pas*. Organizations must be aware of the videos customers (and their own employees) are posting about them—and then manage post haste.

8. *CitySearch*. CitySearch.com is an online city guide that provides information about businesses in the categories of dining, entertainment, retail, travel, and professional services in cities throughout the United States. It's ideal for people who have just moved to a city or for tourists and visitors to find contact information, maps, directions, and editorial and user reviews for the businesses listed. User reviews operate on a five-star system, and viewers can either indicate that a review was helpful or not helpful. There's also a place to comment on each review.

   CitySearch offers a golden opportunity to begin conversations with customers who are dissatisfied with an experience. But very few businesses respond to user reviews on the site, which represents a missed opportunity to rescue potentially lost customers and have a positive impact on your brand.

9. *Yelp*. With more than 25 million visits each month, Yelp.com is a valuable resource for individuals looking for recommendations of professional services, medical services, nightlife, restaurants, travel, entertainment, and countless other options. The difference between Yelp and CitySearch is that Yelp offers a suite of free tools for business owners to communicate with their customers, privately and publicly; track how many people view a business page; add photos, a detailed business description, up-to-date information, history, and specialties; announce special offers and upcoming events or recommend other businesses. Chapter 7 offers more detail on how Yelp recommends that business owners respond to both positive and negative reviews.

10. *Twitter.* Twitter remains one of the fastest-growing micro-blogging applications on the Web. Emarketer.com projects 18.1 million users by 2010, which is 10 percent of the adult Internet market. What makes Twitter so valuable is that it's one of the true "opt-in" experiences. When a customer takes time to follow you, it sends a message you need to consider. Because of its opt-in nature, customers are truly interested in making a connection with what you say, offer, or demonstrate in terms of customer value. It should be noted that the Millennium generation hasn't really glommed on to this newest craze. Although most do have Twitter accounts, they're rarely active.

However, as we have documented throughout this book, many organizations are embracing this newest entry in the social media realm and are attempting to connect one-on-one with their customers in ways that best suit customer needs. Time will tell what type of long-term impact Twitter will have on the customer service industry.

11. *Blogs.* In 2008, the Internet search engine for blogs, Technorati, reported 112.8 million blogs. That's a lot of blogging—and a lot of opinions being tossed about. There are personal blogs, corporate blogs, political blogs, cooking blogs—you name it, there's a blog for it. One of the advantages of blogging is that blog followers are able to leave comments and feedback on an original post. And let's face it, just as with YouTube, a negative service experience can go viral via influential bloggers in a matter of hours.

Pampered Pooch Playground Applies Social Media

Entrepreneur and business owner Keith Miller loves dogs. So much so that he and his wife started Pampered Pooch Playground (PPP) 18 months ago in St. Louis Park, Minnesota, after a year of thoughtful planning and preparation. The business is targeted to social, nonaggressive dogs that need to be walked, played with, rubbed, and fed during the day while the dogs' "parents" are working. Additionally, the business offers overnight or longer-term boarding and "spa" services. Wondering if the business was a crazy idea when only four dogs showed up the first week, the Millers persevered. Using every marketing method that seemed reasonable—Google, Yelp, Bing, and Facebook—the business steadily grew. According to Miller, "Yelp offers our best return. We probably get two to three new customers per week from that site alone. We do offer a coupon for $10 off the first visit that's generated by Yelp." How does he track how customers find PPP? The enrollment form asks the open-ended question, "How did you learn about us?" Miller says he can tell which sites customers reviewed based on their conversations. He regularly changes his Google ads to be fresh and timely, even seasonal. In the summer months, PPP focuses more on day care; at the holidays, more on boarding.

With the business growing to caring for 65 to 70 dogs daily, Miller wonders how much more he can handle. He and his staff recognize that when the "customer" is happy, the "parents" are happy. To ensure that the dog owners stay happy, he offers a variety of ways to keep them informed. There are web cams for daily viewing of dog activities, Tweets to owners with updates, posts on Facebook with dogs' pictures, and a nightly blog posting about the day's happenings. Miller indicates that some pet owners even get a bit out of sorts when their pooch isn't included in the blog or doesn't make the "featured dog" write-up. "It's important to go where your customer is," says Miller. "One pet owner makes her day care reservations via tweets. In response, we send her regular tweet updates."

(continued)

(*Continued*)

Beyond keeping his dog customers happy, Miller recognizes the importance of a great staff. "First we start with hiring the right people. They absolutely have to like dogs! Then we really try to take care of them. At after-hours staff meetings, we have pizza. We regularly ask for ideas, suggestions, and input to improve things. If someone picks up a last-minute shift or covers for a colleague, we give them a gift certificate to show our appreciation."

When it comes to customer reviews of his business, Miller loves and even encourages them. "Certainly the five-star reviews are what we strive for. But it's okay when we see one that isn't so great. We reach out to each and every person who writes a review at any level. When the review doesn't meet our level of service, we move immediately to try to make it right by the customer."

He gives one example concerning a semiregular customer. Her original five-star rating dropped to four stars based on an incident she had with an employee. Spotting the review, Miller immediately contacted her, sought out more information, and addressed the problem; he offered a free day of care for her beagle. The customer was so impressed by his actions that she updated her review to include his gesture and confirmed that she was now a truly loyal customer.

Miller says he likes to keep the reviews fresh on his site. As a customer review connoisseur himself, he regularly searches reviews. "If I see reviews from only six months to a year ago for a business, I wonder if the information is relevant now," he says. "That's why I like to have reviews for PPP be current. It tells people that you are maintaining the level of service consistently. That's really important."

As the business owner, Miller personally responds to all the reviews he sees, and he checks his sites weekly for updates.

His analysis of click-throughs and customer activity helps him decide what online channels to focus on for marketing and communication purposes.

"There's no point in having it out there if you can't follow up," he says. "I make sure I can respond to all our reviews by limiting my coverage. It's working. I'm very pleased."

We keep saying it, perhaps ad nauseam, but organizations must Pay Attention to what's being said about them in these venues or risk having reputations smudged or even dragged through the mud without any countering efforts. Monitoring blog sites is yet another medium to add to that mix.

Specific services such as Twitter or Facebook may come and go over time. But one thing is certain: People will always have a need to connect around similar interests or buying needs, and the next generation of social networks will likely make it even easier for users to share opinions and experiences from a variety of mobile devices.

Wherever your customers congregate in the future, it's important that you be there, listening, observing, and offering advice where it makes sense. Being engaged is the best way to build goodwill, keep abreast of customer perception, and create credible advocates for your brand.

Pay Attention to the Ways Customers Speak

The voice of the customer ranges from the "shot heard 'round the world" to something so soft, we might miss it. Customers today are talking with their feet, their credit cards, and their clicks when deciding where to take their business. Consider your own experience. What has prompted you to change a provider, try a different entertainment source, or just give up on a favorite vendor? Or perhaps the opposite is true. You so enjoyed your meal, appreciated the extra effort a sales associate made, had a return go better than you could have imagined, or were so wowed by a new product purchase that you just had to tell everyone. The most positive way customers speak is by giving your business their loyal and undying patronage. As we have indicated in previous chapters, to achieve this level a company must prove time after time after time that they deliver a caring, value-added, time-sensitive level of service that sticks out in the customer's mind.

It is likely that with this type of "attraction" the customer will bring additional customers through personal reference and patronage. What more can a business ask? Repeat business— retaining the customers you have—is the most cost-effective way to do business. The challenge is getting there. And when you do get there, the next challenge is staying there. Do not think you can rest on past accomplishments. There is likely to be an upstart company on your heels, waiting for you to falter.

When a customer posts a positive review about your business on a web site—yours or a public one—it is a powerful commentary on how they feel about your organization. When they take time to put fingers to keyboard, it sends a message to others about the impression you've made on them. You have put all the pieces together. Now, truth be told, there are some businesses that incent their customers to write reviews. There are also customers who write a positive review in the hopes of getting something positive in return. But they represent the minority. In reviewing site after site, we have found the more genuine reviews seem to shine through.

When there are positive reviews, build on the feedback. Link a positive review with a specific product promotion or feature on your corporate web site. When writing an e-newsletter or marketing e-mails, you might choose to spotlight a number of favorable reviews with some metric that appeals to the reader; 97 percent of customers prefer the ZX model over the YM model. You can still do statement inserts where you have the option to highlight some specific feedback you received and how that feedback made an impact on your organization. Did someone get an award as a result of the feedback? Did you make something available to customers as a result of feedback? This presents a great way to get creative and to target your audience. And certainly, if you can identify the submission, it's a perfect time to say "thank you" to the customer—publicly and/or privately.

In our own research, 72 percent of respondents indicate that a positive review has a significant influence on decision making. Furthermore, most said that they appreciate finding informative reviews, whether on a product site or a more general site. This same group of respondents said they leave a review hoping to help others who are searching.

Certainly both of these options—customer patronage or reviews—may go in the opposite direction, too. Regardless of the nature of the customer speak, these are gifts to be embraced by organizations and never taken for granted.

Perhaps the most frustrating situation is when the customer does nothing—no repeat business, no positive or negative feedback, no clues of any kind. It's likely their service experience was ordinary or worse, and there is no reason for them to go out of their way to comment about it one way or another. In other cases, customers choose to do nothing because the perception is that a business won't take their feedback seriously. Customers don't trust that when they speak, the organization is listening. Research conducted by Cincinnati-based Convergys suggests that even after a positive outcome (80 percent of customer expectations have been met or exceeded), somewhere in the neighborhood of only 30 percent of those customers will remain loyal to a business. But only 38 percent of customers believe a company will act on their feedback, so they don't take the time to complain or weigh in with an opinion.

But you can't do much to try to "save" customers until you hear from them about what's causing their dissatisfaction or driving them away. That's why it's important to find ways to make it easier for customers to voice an opinion. Then, when analysis or investigation suggests a need for improvement, act on that feedback so that customers know you're taking it seriously.

Convergys shares some interesting numbers around customer speak and the power of the Internet, customer review sites, and beyond:

- It is anticipated that within the next three years there will be 115 million people who will *create* content on web sites.
- An estimated 155 million people are anticipated to *consume* content in the next three years.
- It's estimated that YouTube has reached 1 billion views per day—all since its inception in February 2005.

Generational differences also play a role in customer speak. It's no secret that the Millennial generation, those born between 1980 and 2001, has taken to phone apps, texting, instant messaging, blogging, and other alternative methodology in addition to the more traditional methods when they're the only option available. In Figure 5.1, Convergys shows how the predominant generations (Boomers, Gen-Xers, and Millennials) are interacting with organizations compared to how they would prefer to interact if given the choice.

As you can see from Figure 5.1, phone contact still wins out across the board. There is the assumption that when customers reach a knowledgeable, empowered service associate in a company, their needs are more likely to be met than through alternative mediums. This is, of course, dependent on the nature of the need. The financial and cellular service industries, among others, provide a variety of applications for accessing basic information that does not require human contact (particularly interactive voice response, or IVR, and speech recognition and texting). We anticipate that many more customers will be gravitating toward these applications in the years ahead.

When it comes to more complex, private, or detailed information, customers still prefer the human touch. There's just

	How Customers Interact		How Customers Prefer to Interact
E-Mail	Boomers	12%	6%
	Xers	16%	9%
	Millennials	15%	5%
Phone (automated)	Boomers	18%	
	Xers	24%	
	Millennials	25%	Boomers 76%
Phone (Person)	Boomers	53%	Xers 65%
	Xers	54%	Millennials 56%
	Millennials	55%	
Web Site (self service or web chat)	Boomers	35%	13%
	Xers	37%	20%
	Millennials	35%	29%
In Person	Boomers	43%	NA
	Xers	45%	NA
	Millennials	44%	NA
IVR or Speech Recognition	Boomers		6%
	Xers		5%
	Millennials		10%

Figure 5.1   Customer Interaction Preferences by Generation
Source: Convergys, 2008.

something about talking live with a person across a phone line, knowing that he or she is looking at the same information you're looking at, confirming that they understand your situation, and providing immediate information to your question that will always appeal to customers, regardless of their age.

Although many organizations have made the reduction of toll-free-number expenses a top priority by limiting customer access to live service reps, others such as Netflix and Zappos understand the power of the human touch. They have made strategic decisions to shift more resources from Web-based to phone-based customer support.

Every organization is faced with balancing cost against customer satisfaction. Understanding how, why, and when customers prefer to communicate with you will help you choose a mix of contact channels that meet customer needs while also keeping costs manageable.

To meet the changing communication demands of your customers, it will be critical to hire staff that matches the skills of your customer. The more knowledgeable your staff in interpersonal skills, applications, and the products and services you offer, the better the experience for the customer. At REI, the purveyor of outdoor gear, customers who call or e-mail usually get from-the-trenches advice from specialists who actually have used the camping stoves, rain parkas, kayaks, hiking boots, or skis customers are eyeing online.

All the customer service employees at sports e-tailer Fogdog.com hold the title of service consultant. Fogdog believes that stringent hiring criteria are one reason Fogdog's been able to pull off its generalist approach to handling customer inquiries. They may pay more to get the best, but they expect more. Net: You can staff to handle your simplest customer inquiries and problems or you can staff to handle the most complex. Make that decision based on what will enhance your brand reputation, draw customers back again, and work with the variety of communication mediums your customers use, not on cost alone.

When a customer decides to take her business to the competition, she speaks loud and clear. Jean, a woman we know who pampers herself with nail treatments on a regular basis, finally decided to make a change. She reported that she pondered the decision for months. After years of patronage at one salon, Jean was frustrated by the inconsistent quality of the products. She thoroughly enjoyed her nail technician, the ambience of the salon, and the convenience it offered. But she still wasn't satisfied.

Getting a referral from a friend, Jean made the call for a "test" run at a new salon. Pleased with the outcome, she made the decision to switch salons. In this case, Jean found a better product that met her needs. Although making the decision to move was a long process, it finally happened.

What is prompting your customer to make a change? Is it product? Is it price? Or is it the process the customer goes through to do business with you? In an earlier chapter we discussed the

ETDBW concept—being easy to do business with. Repeatedly, customers tell us it's the process that drives them away. Often it's an employee who can't answer a question, isn't empowered, or is completely indifferent. Or perhaps a web site is cumbersome, takes too long to navigate, or doesn't have important information easily accessible. Regardless, the customer begins spending less with you and eventually could be gone. Because it's less costly and more profitable to keep existing customers than to constantly troll for new ones, it's essential that organizations know why customers give up on them.

Customers also speak through decisions they make *not* to spend their money with you. That can include "checking out" items on e-commerce sites but abandoning a shopping cart before pulling the trigger; trying on multiple items in the fitting room and buying nothing; reading reviews of your products and services online and never pursuing the purchase. For whatever reason, the customer loses interest. These decisions can be the result of product price, cost of shipping, selection, ease of transaction, tangible evidence of an organization's attention to service—cleanliness, smell, lighting, and so on, or availability or ease of information or interaction.

The vast amount of data on the Web also allows customers to keep organizations honest in ways that were previously unattainable. When buying a new, pre-owned car, Ann narrowed her selection to one vehicle: a Hyundai. Reaching an agreement with the dealership on a purchase price and delivery date, she sealed the deal. Or so the dealership thought. On delivery of the vehicle, Ann and her husband embarked on a test drive, excited to put the car through its paces. Just minutes into the test drive, both heard and felt a vibration. Speculating on what its cause might be, they returned home and started in on some online research. Web site after web site revealed other car owners with similar concerns.

Armed with information, Ann marched—well, drove—back to the dealership to insist on some corrections. Not wanting to lose the sale, the dealership agreed that they overlooked what should be a simple fix to the situation. Hours later, the problem was solved to the happiness of all concerned.

The way you use product reviews on web sites can also help customers make better buying decisions and in the process boost their satisfaction levels. Muddy Paws Cheesecake in St. Louis Park, Minnesota, offers more than 222 flavors of cheesecake to meet the wide-ranging tastes of its customers. One major source of revenue for the company is its catering service—particularly weddings. In talking with brides about their decision to use Muddy Paws for receptions, they often remark on the positive reviews they've read on the web site, not just about the quality of the cheesecake but also about how easy the company is to work with.

There is no shortage of web sites that give customers a way to speak back and express opinions. If you are a mom or about to be a mom, check out CafeMom.com or TheBump.com. If you want a restaurant review, visit Zagat.com, CitySearch.com, or Yelp.com. If you are looking for car-buying information, check Vehix.com or Edmunds.com. If you want to start creating general blog content, try Sixapart.com or Wordpress.com. For home improvement, there's HGTV.com or TheNest.com.

Most of these sites encourage customer feedback. Visitors can easily pose questions or concerns or leave a comment about a product or service. Customers also can respond to other reviews or comments left by fellow customers.

In July and August 2009, we surveyed more than 300 of our own clients to get their feedback. We asked them this question: *For what reasons have you left a product or service review?* Here's the assortment of responses we received:

- I had a great experience with a product/service   46 percent
- It helps others make a better decision   44 percent
- I had a terrible experience with a product/service   38 percent
- I know how valuable reviews are, so I want to   19 percent
  return the favor
- It helps the business   12 percent
- It's fun   2 percent

As you can see, the intent of reviewers is not just to make their voices heard by organizations but to educate and inform fellow consumers as well. How is your organization Paying Attention to this form of customer speak?

When you visit retail web sites such as BestBuy.com, Target.com, JCPenney.com, Sears.com, or others, comments from customers tend to be product related. For organizations, this can be a gold mine of performance data on things such as product life, durability, usability, value for the price, accessibility, and more. Customers offer gentle and sometimes not-so-gentle hints and tips for others who are considering buying products.

A friend of ours recently purchased a queen-sized inflatable mattress for the rare occasion she had more guests than bed space. A great tip she picked up from customer reviews is to overinflate the mattress to ensure that it stays firm for an entire night's sleep. Not only was she happy to learn this tip, but her guests appreciate it all the more.

Companies also have proven, time and again, that feedback from customers can help improve product design or performance. Thom Miller, president of Hopkins, Minnesota-based Two Rivers, Inc., which sells a line of cookware products, says his businesses have made significant changes based on input from customers. One example involves a private-label cookware line that was discontinued as a result of customer feedback. In repeated reviews, customers complained that the nonstick surface didn't hold up after minimal use. Because the product didn't meet the company standards, it wasn't hard to make the decision to discontinue it. In another situation, customer feedback led to a creative solution. One top-selling brand of cookware was designed in such a way that the handles became very hot on the stove. A retailer verified the comments through its own testing and alerted Miller. Together with the manufacturer, Two Rivers provided a solution that allowed the retailer to continue to carry the cookware without risk of injury to its customers (a handle cover was provided with each purchase). This is just another example of what can happen when an organization takes customer feedback seriously.

Twitter is one of the new channels for customer speak. Tweets are in real time, limited in detail, and evolving. Several major brands or businesses are focusing on Twitter to respond to customer concerns, questions, and comments. Best Buy, for example, developed its "Twelpforce," a large crew of service agents that use the microblogging service to aid customers. According to Barry Judge, Best Buy's chief marketing officer, the Twelpforce has answered over 20,000 customers' questions in the three months since its inception. Comcast also is a pioneer in using Twitter to address customer questions and service-related problems. (See the case study in Chapter 4.)

All the leading players in this genre recommend clear boundaries and expectations for associates who are responding to tweets. They give their associates training on how to deliver a consistent message, demonstrate professionalism, avoid any overt selling, and always remember that what they write is out there for all the world to see.

Based on data referenced earlier in this section, the telephone remains the dominant communication vehicle. But many organizations do whatever they can to keep customers from contacting live service reps. What message are they sending? There is something to be said about that human contact. From the customer's perspective, phone interaction offers the opportunity to get a question answered in detail or a problem resolved in one call, rather than endure a series of back-and-forth e-mail messages.

Years ago, John Naisbett, author of the book *Megatrends*, said, "The more high tech the world becomes, the more people crave high-touch service." We think that notion still holds up today. Service provided via the telephone feels like high-touch to many customers, since talking to live service employees has become such a rarity. Customers speak not only in words but also through their tone, in the types of questions they ask, problems they uncover, and what's not said. Sometimes all they're looking for is a listening ear on the other end of the line. Are you denying them that opportunity or embracing the opportunity to meet that need?

On the flip side, robotic, unengaged, or unprepared service associates may send a customer on to public review sites such as Yelp screaming and complaining if they receive poor service over the phone. Take care to ensure that everyone on the phones is well trained, knowledgeable, and empowered to help customers when they call.

Evaluating Feedback

Once you've taken steps to identify what customers are saying about you and where they're saying it, you're now faced with figuring out what to do with that feedback.

There are several factors to consider when responding to feedback:

- *Consider the source.* Feedback comes in all shapes and sizes, and how you respond will depend in part on who's delivering the message. If you receive negative feedback on a web site from a longtime customer, it should be dealt with immediately. Nothing is more critical to the success of your business than retaining your current customers—especially your most valuable ones. Call them, e-mail them, reach out to them, find out more information on how you can earn back their trust. You need them—and at one point they needed you; you need to make them need you again.

  On the other hand, you may receive a "thumbs-down" from a new or anonymous customer. Such comments are more difficult to respond to in a personal way—and probably not as critical. However, if there is a way to respond, reaching out to find out what went wrong might garner you a new, loyal customer.
- *Watch the tone.* It's inevitable that you'll occasionally receive feedback from an irate customer. Whether it's someone who

has a legitimate gripe or someone who's just had a bad day and is taking it out on your restaurant by venting in symbols (%&#*#@) that there were no salt shakers on the table, it can be tempting to respond in kind—with a written tongue lashing that he'll never forget. But if you give a response like that, the customer will never change his opinion of your establishment and will tell all his friends and associates to never give you a try. The alternative, though difficult, could be effective: Try killing the customer with kindness instead. For example, a quick tweet apologizing for his bad experience and offering a 10 percent discount, should he be willing to give you another try, might be all the incentive he needs. And it might also cause him to blush at his previous overreaction.

- *Quality versus quantity.* We all love to see qualitative feedback written in specific, detailed, and constructive fashion. But unfortunately all customer input doesn't come similarly gift wrapped. That doesn't mean that large volumes of quantitative feedback can't be helpful. Case in point: eBay.com. According to TheBidFloor.com, in 2005 eBay had more than 2.25 million sellers and more than 200 million customers worldwide. With that many individuals vying for business, a large quantity of feedback on sellers can be extremely helpful. A power seller with a feedback rating of 99.8 percent and a total of 14,588 completed transactions ranks as a pretty safe bet. A quick glance at those numbers offers potential bidders assurance that their auction should be successful. If the feedback ranking is lower, customers have the opportunity to read individual feedback comments and base their decisions on more specific information. eBay.com has made it very easy for customers to quickly ascertain the ease of doing business with specific sellers.

- *Consistency of feedback.* Whether it concerns a product or service, a pattern of similar feedback can either encourage or discourage customers when they're making buying decisions. Retailer Amazon.com goes to even greater lengths to provide potential customers with an accurate look at its products. By providing site visitors with the most helpful positive review run side by side with the most helpful negative review," Amazon helps customers get more balanced and credible information to use in making buying decisions. Many customers find this kind of feedback more believable, and thus more useful, than typical marketing pitches companies might use to sell their products. For example, take a look at a similar "positive/negative" customer review approach used with digital cameras:

Most Helpful Favorable Review:
"I purchased this camera just before a 19-day trip to the East Coast and gave it quite a workout ... nearly 2,800 pictures taken during the trip, and only about five of them were unclear due to my unsteady hand. The rest were great, even zoomed out to a ridiculously large size on my computer, with crisp lines and faces, and vivid colors, far exceeding any 35mm or digital camera I have used in the past.

The camera itself and the software included with it are incredibly intuitive. Though there are many manual settings possible, I set the camera in Auto mode and just clicked away. Many places I took pictures required me to turn off the flash, but even those were very clear and bright, and I had to do nothing but aim and shoot.

The delay time between pictures was negligible, and the rechargeable AA batteries I used were good for around 200 pictures a charge, even using flash and with frequent zooming in and out. I used a 16 GB SDHC chip and had the capacity to take 5,000 pictures! I'm still working on filling the first chip!

The provided software is also very simple to use ... as easy as plugging in the provided USB cable and turning the camera on. All pictures are quickly and automatically saved in folders by date, regardless of how many times in a day you download them, and renaming or tagging pictures is a breeze. I have not even begun making full use of the picture touch-up features, but the software includes a fun and easy slideshow application that makes sharing pictures via desktop or projector a snap.

Overall, I could not be happier that I purchased this camera! I look forward to mastering all its features, but as a user-friendly, versatile, and inexpensive point-and-click camera, it blew away all my expectations. It does all that Canon says it does and makes taking pictures fun and easy, right out of the box!"

Most Helpful Critical Review:
"Though the overall quality of this point-and-shoot camera seems good, there are a couple of issues I have with it. I have found that the quality of the photos taken with a flash under fluorescent lights in my garage is lacking a bit. Trying to open the camera to put batteries and/or a card in it is not easy at all. The image stabilizer is not what I thought it would be either, and some movement is detected in the photos when it is used by those not familiar with the camera's operation, such as kids. All this being said, if a person wants a good quality and relatively cheap point-and-shoot camera, they won't go wrong with this model."

Based on the successful use of this product review approach on photography sites, Amazon.com, and other sites, it might make sense to consider adapting it for use on your own web site.

- *Is the feedback realistic and actionable?* Let's face it. Some feedback just needs to be taken with a grain of salt, often because customers have unrealistic expectations. Going into McDonald's and complaining about the lack of linen napkins makes no sense and is quite futile. In addition, some customer feedback is clearly off base or inaccurate, and that's when it makes sense for businesses to step in to clarify the facts. Witness the exchange below from TripAdvisor.com regarding the Best Western Lake Buena Vista Resort Hotel in Orlando, Florida.

Customer Review:
"I booked online with a deal promotion. It was $18 per night. For this price, it is good. The hotel is clean and big enough for 2. Also, it provides a shuttle bus to Disney. (However, only 1 bus in the morning, and 1 in the night for return.)"

Management Response:
"Thank you for submitting a review. Our hotel, located in the Downtown Disney Resort area, doesn't offer rates as low as $18 per night. This may not be the correct hotel as our transportation to all Four Walt Disney World Theme Parks starts one hour before the parks open and runs every 30 minutes up until two hours after the parks close."

- *Focus on customer loyalty drivers.* You can't please everyone. No matter how hard you try, you'll have customers who will never be delighted with the experience they have of your organization. There are always choices that must be made. What demographic are you trying to appeal to the most? Who are your most valuable customers? What service dimensions have the biggest impact on customers' repurchase intentions? How you choose to respond to feedback should be based on these factors and more.

Taking a Closer Look: Glossary of Terms

Throughout the book, we have used terms repeatedly with the assumption that they are well understood. At this point we thought it would be useful to offer some definitions and descriptions related to social media and other new technologies that customers and organizations are using with increasing regularity.

Following are terms we found important to define and clarify:

Web 2.0. A term associated with Internet applications that fosters and encourages interactive information sharing and exchange of dynamic content that reaches well beyond simple information retrieval. A Web 2.0 application becomes a platform that allows users to own and control data, run software through a browser, or possibly add value to the application as they use it. Examples of these applications include social networking sites, blogs, video- or photo-sharing sites, Web-based communities, or business sites.

Analytics. "The science of analysis." A simple and practical definition, however, would be the way an entity (i.e., business) arrives at an optimal or realistic decision based on existing data. According to Wikipedia, business managers may choose to make decisions based on past experiences or rules of thumb, or there might be other qualitative aspects to decision making; but unless there are data involved in the process, it would not be considered analytics. In today's marketing and business context, the term *analytics* often refers to establishing measures against an objective.

Data mining. A term that often refers to the collection and analysis of data. Patterns and trends may be determined through data mining. Data mining is used to profile customers by market segment, capture problem categories, or possibly review what customers are saying about a business, product, or service. Like any other scientific application, the quality of the pattern or trend is dependent on the quality of the data used.

Social networking. Gathering like-minded or interested people into "communities" to explore, discuss, and connect through networks—mostly online. There may be internal networks (a private community within an organization, association, education provider, etc.) or external networks (those open to the public). Social networks increase the sense of community and build a sense of trust on recommendations of participants.

Metrics. A more current term for measures of performance. Also known as *goals* or *objectives*.

Search engine optimization (SEO). The process of increasing the traffic volume to a web site from search engines (Google.com, Bing.com, Ask.com, YouTube.com, Yahoo.com) to improve the standing or increase the rank of that site.

Interactive voice response (IVR). Technology that allows a computer to recognize voice or touchpad input. In the telecommunications industry, IVR is also referred to as the Automated Attendant.

Participative marketing. Describes a shift in focus to engage customers to work with you around a product or service whereby the organization may personalize the marketing efforts to the individual. The more a customer is engaged with a product, the more likely it is that the customer will stay loyal to the brand.

RSS. Most commonly translated as Really Simple Syndication but sometimes Rich Site Summary, RSS is, according to Wikipedia, a family of Web feed formats used to publish frequently updated works—such as blog entries, news headlines, audio, and video—in a standardized format. Organizations use RSS readers (computer applications) to aggregate information being written about them so that they may more easily monitor, track, and respond to that information.

Business Analytics Are Vital

To make customer feedback pay off, it's critical to measure and manage your analytics. Now, when the reach of the customer is extending well beyond the obvious grasp for a typical business, it is perhaps even more important. Remember, your customers are smarter, more time driven, and demanding than ever before. Repeatedly, we have reinforced that a significant differentiator is service. A commitment to service quality without a commitment to standards and measurement is a dedication to lip service, not Pay Attention service. A common denominator among companies with reputations for exceptional service is their bias for setting service standards and their prodigious efforts to measure how well those standards are met.

With the variety of communication vehicles that customers have today, it might seem overwhelming to integrate all this feedback into your measurements. Many of the basic measurements are still vital, but new measurements can be added along with some potentially new tools. It might be helpful to look at broad categories for measurement purposes. These would include functional or operational measures, customer measurement, and adding channel measurement because you are likely to add some of the new communication channels.

Functional measurements focus on the way the business is operating. These may speak to some of the Tangibles or your ETDBW efforts. In addition, they are likely measurements that reflect your marketplace purpose. When you measure against your purpose, it makes it more real to everyone in the organization. For example, if one of your service promises is for timely deliveries on all shipments and your customers have told you that means 24-hour turnaround on all orders, measure that. Remember that there might be a difference between being "on time" and being "timely" in the eyes of your customer. First, the 24-hour standard is *your* technical standard, not the customer's. To the customer, "timely" is a perception, not a measurement, as it is to you. Second, "timely" or "on time" to you typically refers to when the order goes out your door. To customers, those same words may well mean the time the order comes *in* their door, is on the shelf in their warehouse, or is in hand and ready for distribution or use in their system. And because of the power of customer perception, if your customer believes that there is a problem, there is a problem. Your measurement system has to tell you about the problems customer are perceiving as soon as possible, not just comfort you with statistics.

Customer measurement is learning everything you can about your customer. Who are they? What level of involvement do they have with your organization? How engaged is each customer? What is the customer saying about you? In today's environment, there are a variety of tools to assist with these measures. Many of them are free or low cost. Certainly, you will need to weigh the cost/benefit prior to investment. If you are trying to assess engagement, use tools such as Google Analytics or Web analytics. You might want to consider the ratio of comments to posts. For this consider blog analytics. If you are trying to figure out who your influencers are, it might be a measurement of time on your web site or who the repeat customers are. Or to get to the details of your customer mix, you might want to assess mentions of your brand, your product or service, or your competition. In this area, use Google Alerts, blog searches, or possibly incorporate a Net Promoter Score.[1] This compares the positive and enthusiastic recommendations to the negative ones. Or, to learn more about the characteristic behaviors of your audience segments, the Groundswell Profile from Forrester is highly recommended (www.forrester.com/groundswellprofile_tool.html).

Forrester shares an interesting graphic about audience that shows the breakdown by generation of who creates content or comments on, joins in, or watches content. The influence in the social media is more significant across generations than you might think. Generational differences do apply, but it's enlightening to see how each is taking to the social networking scene. Figure 5.2 shows how participation—of those who create content or join

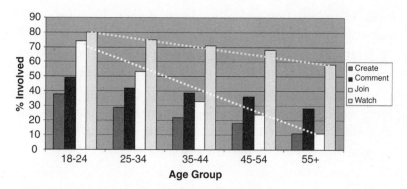

Figure 5.2   Social Media Behavior by Generation
Source: Forrester/Groundswell Profiler.

in—might drop off as we move through the generations, but those who are watching stays very high and consistent over the years. Older consumers obviously are significantly influenced by what's happening. If you have a mainstream customer base, you should be sure to include all market segments. Older customers are certainly influenced by social media and are likely to move there, albeit more deliberately.

The last form of measurement may involve your channel applications. You might be able to count which channel garners the biggest response. If you want to automate this process, a good bet may be BudURL – a basic free program. By selecting a specific link and including it in both an e-newsletter and a tweet, for example, this system will track where the responses come from. Certainly, a great way to track response. The dimension of channel measurement is that of consistency. Closely review delivery, information, and contact rates for consistent high levels of service.

Regardless of what you decide to measure, remember to keep looking at your data from the customer's perspective. Always try to shift the numbers around and consider the impact from the outside in.

Managing the Moments of Truth

In every organization and with every customer, there are critical points of interaction. We call these Moments of Truth (MOT). At each MOT, a customer may form a perception of or evaluate your service. Figuring out which of these MOTs is the most important to customers—which have the biggest impact on their satisfaction levels and, more important, their repurchase intentions—can help you determine where to measure, improve, and change.

Some questions you may want to consider are:

- What do your customers care about? What factors weigh most heavily in determining their repurchase intentions? What are their biggest "pain points"?

- What are customers saying about what they care about – to you, on web sites or social networks?
- What else do customers find "talk-worthy"?
- Will your customers recommend you to others? If no, why not?

When you look at things from the customer's point of view, you may come to realize it's been some time since you have assessed how you do things from "the outside looking in." Are you doing the same old, same old because it's easy and expedient but perhaps not the most effective or customer friendly? Are you focused only on controlling cost without factoring in effects on customer satisfaction or future loyalty?

Consider customer service metrics, for example. Many organizations measure things like talk time, number of rings to answer, or call abandonment. In today's environment, customers tell us over and over again that what they value most is reaching a knowledgeable employee who can answer the question, solve the problem, or clear up an issue in the first call.

It may take more than the allotted three minutes to listen completely and carefully to the customer, and to be sure the service associate is answering the correct question or gathering all the relevant information. The customer doesn't care how many calls you answer in a day or how fast the phone is answered. What he wants is someone who can help him. Are you measuring the right things? Perhaps you should be measuring one contact resolution, exceeding customer expectations or customer retention.

There are multiple ways to assess and analyze these Moments of Truth. You may choose to look at the functional or operational side. You may choose to review the various channels of contact. Or, you may choose to review the perspective of value-added for the customer. All have merit. Selecting one, or all, and establishing specific measures moves you along the path to create a baseline of data. Identifying this baseline is critical before making any improvements or changes. When you start to measure, you will have a point of reference for comparison. It may take several months to gather the data and create your baseline, but it is an essential step.

As you move through this process, you will become more sophisticated in how you look at the data and refine your metrics. You are likely to start looking at:

- The consistency of Moments of Truth – Does the customer have the same experience with each interaction?
- The consistency of the importance of that moment of truth to each segment of your customer population – What is each segment of your audience telling you about an importance factor? Is it different across segments or similar? How well you perform on specific moments of truth?

When you collect the data and compare it to what your customers are talking about, you will learn where to change, tweak, and eliminate. Consistency of each moment of truth influences how customers will recommend your organization. Certainly, the more consistent my experience, the more confident I am in my recommendation.

Ten Action Steps

Here are 10 steps to get you moving in the direction of Paying Attention to review sites, social media, and other channels where customers likely are spending more time talking about your organization:

1. *Consider your own history as a customer.* How have you engaged in and navigated the world of computers, telecommunications, social networking, business web sites, and the increasing number of "apps" out there? How has your comfort level changed? What new experiences—both positive and negative—have you encountered in the last month or six months?

2. *Make sure you have a good grasp of your purpose, strategy, and core customer.* Internally review all the systems and processes that make up your business. Are they customer friendly and well aligned? Does each piece reinforce the message you want to send?

3. *Build an awareness of your company's online presence.* Consider all the ways your customer may search for your products or services and continually work on search engine optimization tactics. Then make it a practice to search your company or product daily, weekly, biweekly. Look for where your business turns up in search rankings. Look for any mention of your company and if it's unfamiliar, check it out.

4. *Go to where your customers are.* Are they Facebook users? Might they be on Yelp or CitySearch? Start to expand your search to other relevant sources.

5. *Establish a baseline.* Collect any and all data that you can. If the customer says you have great products but it's tough to place an order or the shipping options aren't clear, what does that tell you? Are you ETDBW? What information might be missing to make it easier for the customer to understand or to contact you to ask a question? It's from this baseline that you will be able to measure how changes in strategy or additional channels impact your business.

6. *Establish goals and metrics.* Remember, metrics should be directed to those things that customers say are important. If those values aren't clear, spend some time asking your customer and find out. Then measure, measure, measure. In time you will learn what is important and what is not. Initially it's better to have too much information than too little.

7. *Expand to other channels when you are comfortable doing so—but don't wait too long.* Go thoughtfully. Go to where your customers are. It's better to be in fewer channels and be deeper and do that one or those two things really, really well.

Perhaps start with the free or very low-cost platforms such as Google Alerts or some of the others: Blogpulse, Net Promoter Scores, BudURL, and Scoopler. When you do expand, remember to monitor and measure—frequently and regularly.

8. *Reach out to your customers through social networking.* Respond to both positive and negative comments. Say thank you for each gift of feedback.

9. *When something does go wrong, recover quickly and thoughtfully.* Fix both the person and the problem. Once that mission is accomplished, look internally for where a breakdown indicates that there is a process or moment of truth that needs to be fixed, changed, modified, or eliminated.

10. *Ensure that you have hired the right people for the key roles in your organization.* Reward and reinforce the behaviors you want repeated. When there are acts of extraordinary service, make a big deal of it. Take care of your internal customer as well as or better than your external customer. Remember that you cannot afford to lose your top performers. Celebrate each success.

Make Your Web Site ETDBW

We talked in Chapter 4 about the importance of making your systems ETDBW—easy to do business with. A big part of having ETDBW systems is having a web site that is also ETDBW.

In 2000 we conducted extensive research on what an ETDBW web site should include and how it can be as user-friendly as possible to customers.[2] Obviously, much has changed in the past decade—hence the writing of this book! However, many of those core principles are as relevant today as they were then, or perhaps they serve as a jumping-off point for where we are today. We've captured the top 10 essentials to ensuring a successful Web presence with your customers.

1. *Be useful.* Customers typically don't care about the history of your founder, so don't make that your opening page or even an obvious detour. Customers *do* care about finding a product that fits their needs quickly and easily. Give them easy access to prices, descriptions, and checkouts. Do not inundate them with pop-ups, banner ads, and useless information. Okay, if your founder is an obvious cultural icon— Colonel Sanders, Bill Gates, Dave Thomas, Michael Dell, Steve Jobs, Lillian Vernon, or Steve Case—some voyeuristic visitors might want to read or hear their words of wisdom, even gaze on their visages. Just take care to make that a very minor piece of your Web presence. By and large, customers are at your web site for commerce, not for entertainment.

2. *Make everything obvious.* The best way to do this is to make every vital link and tool accessible on every page. That includes a search field, access to the shopping cart, a direct "jump to checkout" option, shopping categories, contact information, shipping and handling prices, return policies, and customer service. If the buyer has to hunt and search for anything, the experience becomes a burden.

3. *Show them what they've bought.* Access to the shopping cart gives shoppers a sense of security and control. It lets them know what they've chosen and that nothing has been accidentally purchased or lost. A one-click link to the shopping cart is essential to assuring customers that they've purchased what they think they've purchased.

4. *Encourage customers to make contact if they want help or have a question.* Putting a business online doesn't mean you can reduce the customer service experience. In many cases it will increase your need to communicate with customers, and the channels used for that communication will expand. An increase in the number of options you provide for customer communication will usually decrease the cost per transaction but not necessarily your total customer service net. Many sites have gone to "live chat," whereby a customer

may immediately engage a service representative online to ask questions, get clarification, clear up confusion, or simply get help. The live chat option puts the transaction in real time for both customer and organization. The immediacy of the help may in fact save a transaction.

5. *Give consumers access to help on their terms.* Nothing infuriates a Web shopper more than a site that doesn't have contact information and multiple contact options. Your 800 number should be boldly listed on every page. The Contact Us link, which must be accessible on every page, should list phone numbers, addresses, and e-mail addresses for real people who will actually respond. There is nothing more frustrating than going to a Contact Us link and finding only a form to complete to have someone contact you. A single e-mail address to info@address.com also doesn't cut it. Why? There's no accountability! Consumers have very few expectations of getting a response from a generic address. They are more trusting of an actual name.

6. *Answer every e-mail in less than a day.* Better yet, answer an e-mail in less than an hour! And do it in a personable manner. E-customers across all industries expect an acknowledgment of their inquiries within one hour and an actual answer to their questions within 24 hours. Yet our research shows that only 12 percent of customers actually receive an acknowledgment within an hour, and only 43 percent receive one in 24 hours. Don't be the site that lets them down. A friendly, timely, personal, and relevant response makes you stand out from your competition.

7. *Make the site easy to navigate.* Our studies show that regardless of the Web savvy of the user, ease of navigation is the most important element of design. In fact, the more savvy users have greater expectations of site navigation because they know what the Web is capable of. The Web is not a linear experience. Users will not travel through departments to find what they want. Sites that offer tabs and simple navigation design make jumping around easy and efficient.

8. *Put a price with every product.* Consumers want to comparison shop, so prices should be up front and everywhere. List them next to every initial product link and again with the product description. Don't make shoppers drill to the description to find out what a product costs. This wastes their time, which is counterproductive.

9. *Tell customers how they can return items, and make it simple.* If you operate a bricks-and-mortar as well as a clicks-and-mortar store system, let customers return merchandise to any of your locations. If you are a dot-com, include a return label and return shipping instructions with the package so that if something is wrong with the order, the customer can simply retape the shipping box and leave it for the postal carrier. Many organizations are following the lead of Zappos.com and offering both free shipping and return shipping, should that be necessary.

10. *Deliver products on time.* If you tell a customer a product will arrive on Tuesday, it had better arrive on Tuesday—or even Monday! To avoid disappointing customers or potentially seeing an exposé on Youtube.com, either deliver products in the amount of time promised—and keep your customers updated as to when and how an item was shipped—or explain in detail at your site when an item can be expected to arrive.

Weighing the Pros and Cons

We've talked a lot in this chapter about the various options for customers to communicate with us and different venues for choosing to leave feedback. However, customers' main options for leaving feedback via the Internet are threefold: your web site, a global web site, or a social networking site.

Figure 5.3 shows a chart that details the pros and cons to you, the organization, for each of these options.

Internet Option	Pro	Con
Your Web Site	• More apt to see the feedback and be able to respond • Easier to respond quickly • Feedback is contained to one site • Able to garner referrals • Able to solicit feedback • Easier to collect data • Easier to make quick changes based on feedback • Greater control of an issue • Able to create communities where customers help each other	• Must keep updated • Requires staff and resources to monitor and respond • Feedback is widespread • Customers may tell you what they think you want to hear
Global Web Site	• Minimal expense • Visitors may be more honest • Exposed to more customers • More believable • Can measure content • Able to identify influencers • Could build positive product/service perception • May build organically	• Need staff to monitor • Feedback may also be incorrect or vicious • Exposure to more customers • More difficult to contain • May lose control of brand identity • Could build negative product/service perception
Social Network Sites	• Customers feel like they can build their social capital • More public • Allows for other customers to respond or comment • Trust in what members say • Builds organically • Able to identify influencers • Can measure content • Virtual meeting place—no time or space boundaries	• More public • Potential to go viral • Lose control of brand identity • Could create negative product/service perception • Time to keep community vibrant and alive • Can't control vicious comments • Privacy or identity theft concerns for participants

Figure 5.3 Pros and Cons of Internet Communication Channels

Chapter 6

PAY ATTENTION TO YOUR REACTION

I t wasn't long ago that responding to customer feedback was a straightforward exercise. Customers would phone a call center, fire off an e-mail, or offer in-person feedback when they sought to contact you with a problem or weigh in on the quality of your products or services. Given the limited number of feedback channels, the process did little to disturb the slumber of most service managers, largely because they felt a good measure of control over it.

That, of course, is a bygone era. With the proliferation of social networks, customer review sites such as Yelp, Yahoo! Local, CitySearch, and the growing number of discussion boards used by companies on their own web sites, millions of customer opinions, ranging from enthusiastic kudos or angry diatribes to ideas for improvement, are floating around cyberspace at any given moment. In fact, today's organizations receive so much feedback about their service quality on the Web that many have ceased hiring secret shoppers to measure it.

There's little doubt that more and more consumers are searching for your business via Web browsers—and then leaving comments about the quality of their experiences once they've done business with you. A study co-authored by comScore and the Yellow Pages Association found that local searches for businesses, products, and services grew 58 percent in 2008 and totaled some 15.7 billion searches.

There's also little debate about how much impact those online compliments or rants have when read by others pondering doing business with you. According to a survey by the Opinion Research Corporation, 84 percent of Americans say that online reviews influence their purchasing decisions. In fact, a body of research shows that customers don't trust e-commerce sites that lack customer reviews as much as they do sites that encourage them. Apparently a failure to encourage free speech about your product or service quality makes many customers believe you have something to hide.

This explosion in new ways for customers to speak out about your business also presents a daunting challenge: how best to corral and address the avalanche of comments in ways that positively influence customer perception—and more important, future buying intentions?

Ignore at Your Peril

We've seen the damage that can be done to organizations that choose to ignore or shrug off the social media phenomenon, many believing that customer comments won't have an impact beyond individual web sites or that they're too off-base or overly dramatic to warrant a response.

In 2008, Target Corp., the Minneapolis-based retailer, found out the hard way how ignoring a segment of its customer base can wound its corporate reputation. The founder of a blog called ShapingYouth.org called Target complaining about a newly released advertising campaign that showed a woman lying across a big target pattern (the retailer's logo) with the bull's eye located at her crotch. The blogger, Amy Jussel, wrote the company to say "targeting crotches with a bulls-eye isn't the message we should be putting out there."

Target's public relations team sent back this e-mail response: "Unfortunately we are unable to respond to your inquiry because Target does not participate with nontraditional media outlets. This practice is in place to allow us to focus on publications that reach our core guest."

Details of the snub quickly spread on the Web, and the reaction from the blogosphere was immediate—and heated. Target came under widespread attack for ignoring the online user community, a good portion of whom are loyal Target customers. A headline on the web site for the Word of Mouth Marketing Association stated that "Target doesn't participate in new media channels?"

Blogger Jussel herself was far from impressed: "Any customer deserves a response to a concern, so I found this to be a shortsighted, ill-conceived judgment call," she told *The New York Times*.[1]

There's also a new reality at play when it comes to acknowledging customer reviews left on web sites. Consider a customer who moves to a new city, uses Google to search for dry cleaners in his immediate area, gets a list of 10 businesses, then starts by clicking on the first business listed. If that site lists only two customer reviews—and both are negative—and the dry cleaner in question hasn't bothered to respond to the reviews, the browsing customer is likely to simply move on.

Monitoring what's being said about you online, then taking time to respond where appropriate is critical in today's business environment, where more customers than ever factor the give-and-take on review boards into their buying decisions.

We've also seen companies that *do* respond appropriately to online feedback but at the speed of an old response paradigm, not with the lightning-quick reactions needed on today's Internet. In Chapter 1 we detailed the pain experienced by Domino's Pizza when two of its employees posted a prank video on YouTube showing them doing unsavory things with food products and putting those items on customers' sandwiches.

While Domino's top brass ultimately responded to the fiasco in an admirable way—Domino's president posted his own video on YouTube apologizing for the prank—the response came after much of the damage had been done. Had Domino's assigned staff to more actively monitor Web traffic or perhaps used more monitoring tools to scan for online references to the company, it might have been able to pull the YouTube video earlier and better contain the situation.

Tracking What They're Saying

At this point you might be asking, "We'd like to pay more attention to what customers are saying about us online, but there is oodles of feedback, and we don't have a staff or budget big enough to dedicate to monitoring comments. How do we get a handle on it?"

The good news is there are plenty of cost-effective ways to manage what on its face might seem an overwhelming task: tracking references to your company or products in the online universe. Many new monitoring tools, some free and others fee-based, have emerged to help you with the task of scouring blogs, web sites, video-sharing sites, and the like for mention of your company or its brands.

A small sample includes the following: Google Alerts, a free service that provides e-mail or RSS alerts when your business is mentioned in a review or blog; Backtype, which monitors how people respond to your company's blog posts; Twitter Search or Tweet Deck, which monitors real-time customer feedback; Technorati, among the biggest blog search engines; and the "dashboard" tool on the review site Yelp.com, which enables business owners to track their page views and promote their products.

There also are paid services such as Radian6 for tracking and listening to customers on social media.

In addition, vendors such as PowerReviews, Bazaarvoice, and Biz Rate have the express purpose of helping companies collect, structure, and moderate online customer reviews. A search for online reputation management vendors will turn up more such suppliers.

Whoever you decide to partner with, the idea is to stay on top of what's being said about you online, lest isolated brush fires blow up into raging conflagrations.

To Engage or Not to Engage?

Once you've identified what's being said about you online and where most of that discussion is occurring, you face a weighty decision: whether to react to the customer commentary. You might think this is an easy choice, given the conventional wisdom that *all* customer feedback—particularly where problems or service breakdowns are concerned—deserves some level of response. As a customer service executive at a Fortune 500 company once told us: "If a customer believes he has a problem, he has a problem. Period."

But not all negative feedback is created equal. Although deftly addressing some complaints or issues can convince would-be defectors to give your company a second chance or cease using the online megaphone for further trash talking, in other cases jumping into the fray can be like throwing gas on a fire.

For example, customer reviews that feature overly dramatic words and no hint of constructive criticism—a customer who asks an Internet service provider to "Please make my connection faster than a hand crank" or a hotel customer who writes "Your bartenders are unbelievably arrogant, your management beyond inept and your food not fit for a wild dog" — might not be worth a public response on channels such as Twitter or Facebook, given that the odds of rational or productive discourse with such a customer are small. Some customers are simply mad at the world and wouldn't be happy in Nirvana.

It's also vital to refrain from responding when you're in an angry state. Most of us are proud of our organizations, and negative comments can feel like a blow to the solar plexus. Give yourself a timeout to reflect after reading bad reviews and take a breath before returning to the keyboard and engaging. You'll almost always respond in a more balanced, professional, and constructive way after getting a bit of perspective.

Here are some guidelines for when you should respond to customer comments or reviews posted online, whether they are less than glowing or of the positive variety:

- *When you've obviously erred.* Sometimes your company has clearly messed up. When a repairman arrives hours late, a financial statement has errors, or a shipped product arrives damaged or with parts missing, you need to jump online and make amends to customers who complain. This means apologizing for the error, offering to fix the problem, and in some cases providing atonement for the breakdown—whether it's a coupon, a waived shipping charge, or some other way to let customers know you feel their pain. It also means making a promise to improve next time around. (For more detail on crafting proper responses in public or private settings, see Chapter 7.)
- *When a negative review shows signs of going viral.* It's tempting to sit back and do nothing if you think a negative review or opinion is wildly off base or written on what you think is an obscure blog with limited readership. But as we've seen time and again, what appear to be isolated cases of service problems tucked away in the far corners of the Internet can quickly blow up and spread like wildfire,

becoming YouTube sensations and garnering millions of hits overnight.

Some companies, such as Dell Computer, are constantly subject to rumors about things like new product development. Responding to that type of rumor does little good. But if you're seeing a trend of negative comments about particular product or service issues on review sites and many others are jumping in with "they burned me, too" responses, that's a signal to take a deep breath, investigate, and try to contain the damage. Listening without reacting, keeping an open mind, and avoiding excuses or defensiveness are keys to resolving these situations.

- *If customers are misrepresenting your products or services*—what a warranty offers or what your current prices are or if they're trashing the buffalo burger they ordered at your restaurant when there is no such item on your menu—you'll want to gracefully step in and state the facts.

  We recommend you try to first address these comments through a private e-mail or message to the reviewer, if possible. If you feel it is important to post publicly to clear up confusion, don't attack the reviewer or get involved in "He said, she said." Simply point out information that can be proven true, and be polite and straightforward.

- *When the reviews are positive.* You might think there's little need to follow up on positive reviews, but responding can have multiple benefits. Your goal here should be only to deliver a simple thank-you and let the reviewer know you appreciate the time they took to comment. That can only increase the odds that they'll stay loyal to you in the future.

  What you don't want to do is follow up with gift certificates, offers to provide further testimonials, requests to be on mailing lists, or anything else that suggests tit-for-tat for having provided the review; reviewers don't appreciate feeling bribed for having written something good about you. And above all, don't try to sell them additional products in this context. Simple, short, and grateful is best. Offer anything beyond that and you can defeat the purpose of contacting the reviewer.

How Whole Foods Addressed an Online Uprising

It's not unusual for an organization's leaders to say or do something that causes a segment of the customer base to grab its proverbial pitchforks and storm the corporate gates. That was the situation faced by grocer Whole Foods following an op-ed column that its CEO John Mackey wrote for *The Wall Street Journal*. What makes this case different is that the uprising largely happened in online forums, forcing Whole Foods to react quickly or face a fast-spreading storm of Internet criticism.

In the column Mackey argued for health care savings accounts and declared that health care is not an intrinsic right. The comments, which had a conservative flavor, sent much of the company's liberal customer base into a tizzy. The CEO came under withering fire from the blogosphere and social media enthusiasts for taking his personal stand, presumably under the company banner. "Boycott Whole Foods" movements sprang up around the country and within weeks had thousands of members.

How did Whole Foods react to the online conflagration? The company sent letters to customers apologizing for any offense and created a forum on its web site where customers could discuss the issue. It wasn't long before there were some 10,000 posts on that site.

For his part, Mackey later wrote in a blog that the problem was caused in part by the *Journal's* choice of headline, which read, "The Whole Foods Alternative to ObamaCare," noting that his column never mentioned the President.

The upshot: Whole Foods acted properly by quickly and candidly addressing the situation and by giving customers an online venue for venting about their concerns. By doing so, it limited the issue's shelf life and headed off what could have mushroomed into a bigger phenomenon beyond its web site into the cyber-world at large.[2]

It's also important to know who your key "influencers" are when you're developing a response strategy. As time goes on, the blog commentary or product reviews of certain customers begin to carry more weight with others, owing to the reviewer's credentials, incisive commentary, or subject matter knowledge. Once you've identified those influencers, it pays to do a little extra to try to get them on your side or at least ensure that they have all the data necessary to make good, informed decisions about your organization's products or services.

In the same vein, it's important to separate customer reviews or comments related to your organization's "loyalty drivers"—those service dimensions that weigh more heavily in consumers' decisions to keep doing business with you—from comments about lower-priority service factors. For example, one of a banking organization's identified loyalty drivers might be resolving customer problems on first contact. Any online customer feedback related to that topic might be assigned higher response priority. Conversely, if customers complain about not being greeted with a hello when they enter the bank, management might assign that a lower priority, since customer surveys show that being greeted on arrival is simply a "nice to have," not a deal breaker, when it comes to customers deciding whether to keep doing business with the bank.

Creating Integrated Response Systems

Savvy organizations also regularly monitor social networks, blogs, customer review sites, and discussion boards on their own web sites for signs of emerging problems in product design, manufacturing quality, packaging, distribution systems, and more—as well as new threats from competitors. Many have set up systems to instantly share comment "themes" on social media sites with other parts of their organizations so immediate concerns can be addressed and data compiled on recurring issues or problem references.

When Allsop, a Bellingham, Washington-based company that manufactures computer accessories, noticed a rash of comments on its online discussion boards about problems with product packaging, it quickly investigated and ultimately fixed the problem.[3] Other organizations link customer comments posted on the Web to their call centers, so service representatives can follow up on specific issues or problems referenced online. The pet products company Petco, for example, flags reviews left by displeased customers, forwarding them to service reps who call or e-mail the customer to address the complaints and spread some goodwill.

Rather than sit back and wait for customer comments to trickle in, other organizations are more proactive in soliciting feedback and even new product ideas from customers. In February 2007, for example, Dell Computer launched its now-famous IdeaStorm, a site designed for customers and others to submit ideas for technology or general business improvement. The user community votes for its favorite ideas and demotes ideas they do not like. (For more detail on how IdeaStorm works, see Chapter 7.)

Not only does the process reduce some of the costs of product development, it serves as a large "focus group" and, if a proposed change or product does eventually come to market, Dell has created a group of customers who are likely to be enthusiastic about the product. For example, Dell was getting feedback from many customers who thought the Enter and Apostrophe keys were too close together on the Dell Mini 9 laptop keyboard—so it fixed the problem on the Dell Mini 10. Odds are that customers who suggested the change became fans of the Mini 10.

Traditional Listening Posts

Despite their growing popularity, online channels such as public review sites, social networks, blogs, and review boards on company web sites represent only one way to tune in and listen to the new voice of the customer. In the rush to engage customers flooding the cyber world, it can be easy to overlook or put less stock in traditional, offline listening tools. But capturing a complete picture of the customer experience—keeping your pulse on the shifting needs, wants, and expectations of those who keep you in business—requires more than just reacting to what's being said about you on social media.

A combination of quantitative and qualitative measurement tools—from questionnaires and phone interviews to gathering comments made to front-line associates, sales floor workers, or focus group leaders—gives you that well-rounded feedback. Quantitative measures provide hard data, and qualitative feedback—real, unedited comments from customers about how a service experience made them *feel*—breathes life into the numbers and gives the voice of the customer a more emotional punch. This combination of *fact* and *feeling*-based research is a powerful way to keep current on the customer experience, and when shared with staff—the negative as well as the positive—can keep them motivated to continually improve service quality.

Some of the most relevant and actionable feedback comes from daily one-to-one interactions with your customers. When top management sees its front-line workers as invaluable "canaries in the coal mine"—incenting them to regularly gather, summarize, and share insights, rants, or suggestions gleaned in their daily dealings with customers—it can help eliminate burgeoning service problems while they're still small in scope and provide an early warning system on shifts in customer buying habits.

As the late Ron Zemke, one of the leaders of the service quality revolution and co-author of the seminal book *Service America* once wrote, "Marketplace reality is a fading photograph." Customer needs, wants, and expectations are constantly on the move, adjusting to changing economic conditions, breakthrough technologies, and marketplace trends. When you fail to stay abreast of what consumers are seeking—the total value package that keeps them loyal or makes them start seeking greener pastures—you risk growing obsolete or falling prey to competitors' offerings, a process that often happens in an incremental, even imperceptible, fashion.

We think you would do well to build the listening process around a simple but powerful question: What service factors do you consider most important in doing business with us? Its corollary might be: What can we do to get more of your business?

Not until you know which service dimensions have the biggest influence on customers' repurchase intentions can you begin tailoring survey questions and other listening strategies to those areas—and then funnel resources into fixing any problems in those high-impact areas first. Those "deal breakers" might be an ability for customers to have their problems resolved in one, no-hassle phone or e-mail contact; a guarantee they'll be served quickly and efficiently, each and every time; having a convenient location and hours of business; or being treated with respect and dignity, not as "guilty before proven innocent."

Consider the timeless lessons of British Airways (BA). When the airline sought to upgrade its customer service image, it decided to conduct some market research. The research was aimed at answering two questions: What factors did passengers consider most important in their flying experiences? Second, how did British Airways compare to other airlines on those factors?

Customers said that four service factors stood out from the rest as being vitally important: (1) care and concern on the part of customer contact staff; (2) problem-solving capability of front-line personnel; (3) spontaneity or flexibility in the application of policies and procedures; (4) service recovery, or the ability of front-line staff to make things right when things have gone wrong.

While the first two factors didn't surprise BA executives, the last two—flexibility in applying policy and recovery practices—came out of left field. Customers wanted to know that when a problem arose that didn't fit the rule book, service staff would be creative in finding workarounds to meet customer needs. They also wanted to know that if something went awry, some BA staffer would go out of her way to make amends to customers.

BA management was struck by a disturbing thought: If two of the four key evaluation factors—issues with a big impact on customer loyalty—were things that it hadn't seriously considered, what were the chances that employees were paying attention to them?

Bottom line: When these Moments of Truth go unmanaged and when companies don't take the time to find out what really matters to customers, service can quickly sink to mediocre levels, or worse.

Three Types of Listening

We divide customer listening approaches into three main categories:

1. *Scientific listening.* This is also known as traditional market or customer research and has three objectives. The first is to figure out whether your organization is doing the right things—things that have the greatest impact on customer retention. For example, are you focused on fixing

problems right the first time rather than forcing customers to e-mail or call again and again to get their issues resolved? The second is to figure out whether those "right things" are being done well. The third is to figure out who among current or potential customers agrees with the direction in which you're heading. This form of customer listening can be quantitative or qualitative and can include usability testing, online surveys, focus groups, phone surveys, and the like.

2. *Dramatic listening.* The goal of this type of listening is to demonstrate to customers that you really are listening—and applying the best of their feedback to improving operations—rather than simply going through the motions. Dramatic listening is best done on the front lines, over service counters, on sales floors, and in call centers, where employees should be trained to listen not only for problems but also for those unexpected customer ideas that might spark profitable new services or ways to reduce costs. The key to this type of listening is leaving customers with the feeling of having been heard and having confidence that your company will treat the information received seriously.

3. *Motivational listening.* The most convincing information for leaders is the information they gather themselves. When CEOs, directors, or vice presidents spend time in the trenches, taking a day to handle phones, monitor incoming e-mail or tweets, answer customer questions, or do sales call ride-alongs, they get a more visceral sense of customer needs, problems, and challenges faced by frontline staff.

Experiencing these things directly and personally can make an impact that hours of reading static customer satisfaction reports or listening to data-heavy presentations of service managers in meetings can never approach.

Reacting to Product vs. Service Feedback

How you react to customer feedback on product quality versus service quality dimensions may, on its face, seem similar, but in reality the nature of the transactions requires a different approach that should reflect the more personal and emotional nature of service delivery.

Consider for a moment how you view the purchase of a product such as a refrigerator or a set of car tires versus a service experience such as eating at a fine dining establishment, staying at a hotel while on vacation, or interacting with a business to resolve a mistake on a monthly account statement.

We tend to evaluate many of the products we purchase on factors such as cost, function, reliability, and ease of use. There are exceptions, of course, particularly where it concerns "vanity" purchases. But on balance we have little emotional involvement in most of our day-to-day product purchases.

Customer service scenarios, on the other hand—because they involve more sustained human-to-human interaction—often cause us to respond differently and thus demand that organizations react to service-related feedback in different ways. How we're treated by a call center worker if we phone in to report a service outage, by a bank if we've waited forever in a queue for service, or by hotel staff if the TV in our room isn't working can have bigger impact on our satisfaction (and thus our repurchase or revisit intentions) than whether a commodity product holds up until its stated warranty or performs as promised.

Consider a study done by Professor Jerald Young at the University of Florida that looked at why patients decide to switch doctors. A pre-study presumption was that quality of medical care would be the primary factor influencing such a change, but in fact the research showed that bedside manner was the biggest reason for patient defections to other physicians. Whether patients felt listened to and respected—the quality of service or customer care that the doctor delivered—carried more weight than the equivalent of product quality when it came to patients' future loyalty.

Although customers certainly can and do get upset when products they buy malfunction or fail to meet expectations—and that upset requires redress—how you react to problems they experience in service situations requires a different, escalated level of reaction.

That's because when people treat other people badly, it has a psychological impact with a long shelf life, influencing those who were treated rudely or indifferently for years to come.

Chapter 7

PAY ATTENTION TO YOUR RESPONSE

Every day your employees engage untold number of customers—and potential customers—in person, over the phone, and via e-mail messages, tweets, blog posts, and more. Although the outcome of these individual interactions might not decide your organization's fate, taken as a whole they determine whether your business is perceived as one that values and respects customers or one that views them as a necessary nuisance. Which camp you're placed in means the difference between dollars flowing to or draining from your bottom line.

Service-savvy organizations know that each customer touch-point, whether conducting a mundane transaction or handling a potentially catastrophic problem, is a "moment of truth" that should be approached with the same forethought and care. Certainly some service scenarios, such as those that involve large-dollar, VIP accounts, demand more time and tender loving care than others. But in today's über-networked environment, one wrong move and your indifferent or dismissive treatment of any customer can be retold across the Web or can attract millions of hits on YouTube.

How your people respond to customer questions, problems, product reviews, rants, or kudos is the litmus test of service quality. You can have many of the other right pieces in place—cutting-edge software that tracks mention of your brand across the Internet, tools that solicit customer ideas for product improvements, or value-added services that give clients "warm fuzzies"—but if your customer contact people don't handle those moments of truth deftly, all other efforts to become a service leader are moot.

That's because to the customer, the employee *is* the company in those face-to-face conversations, phone calls, counter-blogging efforts, or responding tweets. Your ornate headquarters building, flashy marketing campaign, cutting-edge technology, or cheerful greeters in your lobby matter little to customers trying to get a vexing problem solved, a difficult question answered, or a tough deal negotiated. All that concerns them in that crucible of service delivery is getting a fast, friendly, and competent response to the issue at hand.

Customer service reputations are won or lost each day in the trenches based on these one-to-one interactions. Get that part right on a consistent basis, and you'll see customer retention rates rise and all-important *word of mouse* grow.

All Eyes on You

Responding to customers in a calm, professional, and service-sensitive way is an art form that takes on even greater importance in public venues such as Twitter or Facebook. Given the absence of nonverbal clues, communicating with customers via e-mail messages, blog responses, tweets, or other channels that rely on the written word is an underrated but high-level service skill that's not easily mastered. It's easy for employees assigned to respond to customer comments on these channels to come off as brusque, unclear, or even defensive to customers. And the stakes are high, since it's not just individual customers who'll see your response on social networks but thousands of other potential customers.

For that reason, companies that are serious about addressing service issues via social media give their people intensive training in how to respond appropriately to multiple scenarios via the written word. Whether via written word, phone, or face-to-face interaction, all the best empathy, listening, and questioning skills still apply.

Half the battle of good service is letting customers be heard. Often customers leave comments on web sites simply because they need to vent or have their side of the story explained. Given the opportunity to voice their opinion, rage or anxiety naturally subsides. Service masters understand that in the majority of cases, it's better to achieve peace with customers than to be proven "right," especially if you want those customers to darken your doorstep again.

On a process level, it's as vital to fix—that is, deal with and reassure—the customer as it is to fix the problem. We explore this *service recovery* process in greater detail in Chapter 8.

Creating Digital Embassies

One way companies are taking their response to another level is by creating so-called *digital embassies*—in essence, places on their own web sites, Twitter, Facebook, and blogs where customers congregate virtually. The idea behind these embassies is to assist customers with questions or concerns about products and services, blog about company developments, and serve as a liaison to the online community. Embassies are designed to be "no-spin zones" where customers can expect straight talk about the company, get a chance to have their voices heard, and have problems looked into and resolved by designated "ambassadors."

Steve Rubel, senior vice president and director of insights for Edelman Digital, a division of Edelman Public Relations that studies how organizations use social media for reputation management, says that well-run embassies prove effective as "listening posts" for gathering information about customers' experiences and creating goodwill by giving customers some insight into management decision making.

Rubel says that the tenor of each embassy depends on the nature of the online community and the resources companies dedicate to running them. For technology-based companies such as Dell, SAP, Amazon.com, or eBay, for example, it might be more vital than others to have a significant presence on social media because more of their customer base trusts and depends on these channels to communicate.

The key to an effective embassy, Rubel says, is choosing the right "ambassador" or social media strategist to be the voice of the company. The role requires not just superior interpersonal and technical skills but also someone who is deeply embedded in the online community. Ambassadors also need to coordinate well with legal departments, corporate communications staff, and brand managers so that those units know what's being said about the company to the social media world.

"Ideally you want to have a corporate 'all-star' of sorts as your ambassador, someone who is already involved in the online community, who understands its sensibilities, who participates regularly and is accepted as one of them," Rubel says.

He points to Frank Eliason of Comcast, noted for launching and guiding the cable company's customer service efforts on Twitter, and Richard Brewer Hay, a full-time blogger for eBay, as examples of effective ambassadors. These two, Rubel says, "live the brand, are service oriented, passionate about their companies, and have earned the respect of the customer communities they serve over time."

Part of the digital embassy concept also includes analyzing online feedback for trends and themes. Many organizations that solicit product reviews on their own web sites, for example, also store them in databases for regular analysis and action. They know the reviews can be a gold mine of business intelligence, providing valuable information on customer demographics, needs, and wants. Business analysts examine these reviews for trends versus previous periods, break down scoring differences between certain customer groups, seek out "themes" in negative or positive reviews, and more.

Indeed, though responding quickly and effectively to customer questions or problems is a critical part of the Pay Attention approach, it's equally important to create a systematic process that regularly analyzes root causes of problems—particularly those that recur or contribute to customer defections—and make changes that create lasting improvements.

Dell Computer: Engaging via Social Media Is "Everyone's Job"

One company that's long employed a version of the digital embassy concept is Dell Computer, a pioneer in the use of social media for customer service purposes. Dell's management believes that listening to and engaging customers on Dell.com, blogs, Facebook, Twitter, and other online communities where they gather is so important it should be a facet of almost every employee's job.

When Dell first began monitoring online conversations in 2006, it assigned a hand-picked "SWAT team" of about 10 technical support specialists, chosen for their mix of interpersonal and technical skills, to use search tools such as Technorati and Google Blogs to scan the blogosphere for any mention of the company, aggregating the comments with an RSS reader. Once relevant chatter was identified, the team would often engage people who posted comments about the company, listening for needs, resolving certain service issues, and sending a message that Dell was now available to help via these channels.

One of Dell's first attempts to reach out to the blogosphere occurred in the aftermath of problems with some laptop batteries in August 2006, which led to the then-largest consumer product recall in history. Dell actively engaged bloggers who were commenting on the recall. In addition, the company's first blog, Direct2Dell, was created at the urging of CEO Michael Dell, who wanted to give customers a place to connect and talk to the company.

One of the company's earliest challenges was convincing Twitter and Facebook users that Dell employees joining their conversations were actually who they said they were. Many users were unbelieving or incredulous that Dell would take the time to engage them in these public forums. But once engaged and assured that Dell employees were authentic, the majority of bloggers and social media users were soon giving the company high marks for its participation and efforts to listen, learn, and help, says Richard Binhammer, Dell's senior manager of corporate affairs.

"I continue to be surprised about how well accepted conducting customer service online is with people who use social media or blogs," Binhammer says. "I came into this thinking customers might be upset that a big company like ours would sort of 'barge into' their online conversations. But our experience is that most have come to welcome that and indeed now expect it in social media."

As its experience with social media deepened, Dell decided to migrate from a centralized service support model to a more dispersed version where employees throughout the company's four divisions now have some level of responsibility for engaging customers via social networks and blogs. Even spending a short period of time each day engaged on those channels helps keep Dell employees connected to their customer base and ensures that they don't become insulated from customer needs or perceptions.

"We came to the conclusion that social media can benefit everybody and anybody in their jobs and that the need to engage and listen to customers cuts across all corporate boundaries and silos," Binhammer says.

Indeed, online customer conversations have become part of how Dell does business, from customer support to product development to marketing. To connect directly with Dell customers on Twitter, for example, Dell employees across departments use a microblogging tool for a variety of business purposes, including answering questions, solving issues, and chatting about technology or Dell initiatives. When the company began using Twitter, it quickly found that users also wanted advice about Dell purchases.

You'll find that the head of Dell's technology and education department, its chief gaming expert, product development managers, the head of its enterprise group, and its liaison with the Linux community all have their own active Twitter accounts.

In addition, Dell people have Twitter accounts connected to Dell Outlet, where the company sells refurbished computers. Employees don't hard-sell the computers on Twitter, but they do talk about the latest inventory and specials and give out coupon codes. Since 2007, Dell has made over $3 million in revenue directly through Twitter, much of it from users of the microblogging site who come to Dell Outlet and then also click over to Dell.com to buy products there.

Rules of Engagement

But where customer service is concerned, just because someone has blogged or tweeted about Dell, that doesn't mean that the company will automatically respond to the missive. For one thing, there's the matter of sheer volume: Dell is mentioned in an estimated 5,000 online conversations every day. One school of thought holds that companies should seek to respond to every complaint or reference to them online, but for most large organizations that's simply not realistic. Most search for themes and trends and respond more selectively to those.

In some conditions Dell will almost always attempt to engage customers online, Binhammer says:

- If there is a clear misrepresentation of the facts in a situation
- If there's a customer service issue Dell knows it can fix

- If a customer's device is still under warranty and if the customer has had a less than positive experience with Dell's call center or there's been another type of service breakdown

"If a customer is blogging about a service experience that doesn't live up to what we like to deliver, we will immediately go in, investigate, and try to make it right," Binhammer says. Like any business, mistakes or a misdiagnosis do occasionally happen, and if they do, Dell trains its technical support staff to apologize, work quickly to fix the problem, and assure customers it won't happen again.

Because of strict customer privacy guidelines, Dell often follows up on service-related comments made about the company in public forums via private e-mail or phone contact, when possible. If someone blogs about a problem they're having with a Dell business laptop, for example, Dell's support staff would first need the customer's identifying information and service tag number to do a proper diagnosis of the issue.

"We can't address those issues in a public forum, because if we do we've violated customer privacy," says Binhammer. So the nitty-gritty of resolving problems often happens away from social media, via phone or e-mail, after an initial contact is made through Twitter or other online venues.

There also are service scenarios in which Dell will opt to stay on the sidelines rather than engage those who've blogged or tweeted about Dell-related issues. Binhammer says employees steer clear of topics with legal ramifications or of rumors concerning new product development. Dell also will usually avoid responding to blogs or tweets about performance issues it knows it can do little to change. For example, a customer with a six-year-old Dell desktop who repeatedly takes Dell to task on his blog for how slow his computer is, which a recent service checkup with the company has shown has a two generations' old processor chip in the hardware, is unlikely to elicit a response.

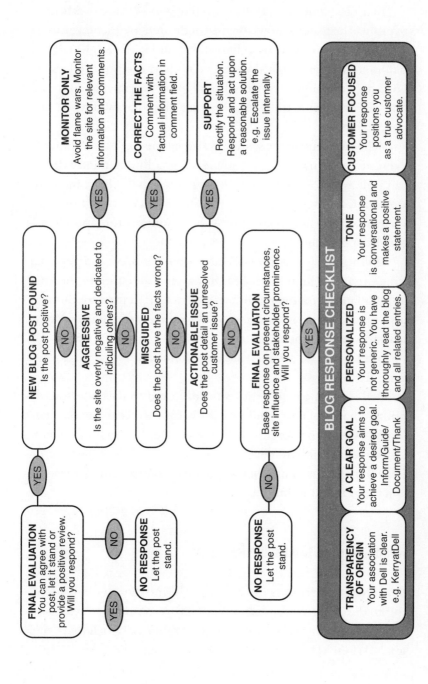

Figure 7.1 Dell Outreach in the Blogosphere

To avoid flame wars, Dell avoids bloggers who are overly negative or whose history shows they are dedicated to ridiculing others.
The "blog assessment" flowchart shown in Figure 7.1, which Binhammer says was inspired by a similar chart used by the U.S. Air
Force to guide online conversations between airmen and the general public, details Dell's strategy regarding responding to blog
posts.

Delivering customer service via social media "is not always an
exercise in saying 'yes' to customers," says Binhammer. While it
can't always give every blogger or Twitter user what they want,
Dell has found, almost without fail, that when it's straightforward
yet empathetic and respectful with customers, the approach is
usually appreciated.

Online dialogue is most effective when it's direct and personal,
which requires high levels of transparency and a more informal
approach than customer contact staff are often used to, Binhammer says. "People in business tend to underestimate the power
of clarifying the facts," he says. "We find our customers usually
respect it when we are up-front with them about what we can and
can't fix for them."

Dell's multipronged efforts to reach out to customers across
online channels have paid dividends for the company on many
levels. One of the biggest is this: Since Dell became involved in
social media, Binhammer says it has seen a nearly 30 percent decline in negative commentary about the company in all networks
and blogs that it monitors.

Responding to Customer Reviews

One area where companies increasingly find themselves responding to customer comments or reviews are on public review sites
such as Yelp, CitySearch, or TripAdvisor that we detailed in Chapter 5. When Yelp gave small business owners the green light to

respond to reviews they thought were incorrect, it represented a turnaround for the review site, which previously hadn't given businesspeople a voice to correct or dispute reviews from customers. Previous to that policy change, Yelp also began allowing business owners to contact people leaving reviews privately.

The shift in policy, though embraced by businesspeople, also opened up a potential can of worms. Yelp wanted business owners only to correct or add factual information to customer reviews, not debate the perceived quality of products or services that customers experienced. That focus acknowledges that customers sometimes get the facts wrong in their reviews. In one case, a reviewer of a Los Angeles restaurant left a review on Yelp stating, "The turkey meatloaf was gritty and cold and I waited 45 minutes for my second $28 margarita." A review of the restaurant menu confirmed that turkey meatloaf was not on the menu that day.

But for owners who've often invested their heart and soul in a business, not responding to a subjective opinion, particularly after a customer has left a particularly nasty review, doesn't come easy. As Yelp cautions on its site, "Contacting reviewers should be approached with care. Internet messaging is a blunt tool, and sometimes good intentions come across badly."

Given the challenge of controlling emotions when responding to reviews, Yelp opted to develop guidelines for review response, advice we think is useful for any organization that solicits product or service reviews on its own web site. And encouraging that feedback is something we strongly encourage, too. Many organizations still shy away from soliciting customer comment or product ratings, frightened that they'll get a lot of negative commentary. In fact, a recent survey conducted by Market Metrix and TripAdvisor found that 85 percent of hotels have no guidelines for monitoring, responding to, or acting on reviews left by guests. In addition, TripAdvisor research found that only 4 percent of negative reviews left on sites were responded to by the relevant organizations.

That represents a big missed opportunity, because only when you know customers are unhappy do you have a chance to keep them before they silently slip away to competitors or they start to use your services less frequently. In addition, research also shows that customers tend to trust companies that solicit reviews of their products or services on web sites more than organizations that don't.

The following is a summary of Yelp's advice to business owners on responding to both negative and public reviews in private—advice we think has application for how you respond to reviews posted on your own web site (see Figures 7.2 and 7.3).

Responding to Negative Reviews

Yelp's advice:

> There's no doubt that responding to negative reviews is hard. Before responding to a negative review, take a deep breath and think carefully about what you are going to write. Negative reviews can feel like a punch in the gut. It hurts when someone

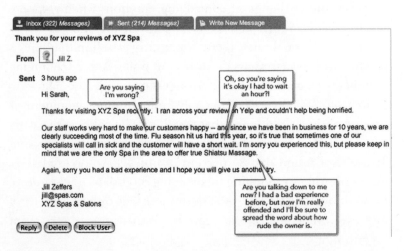

Figure 7.2 What *Not* to Do When Responding to Negative Reviews

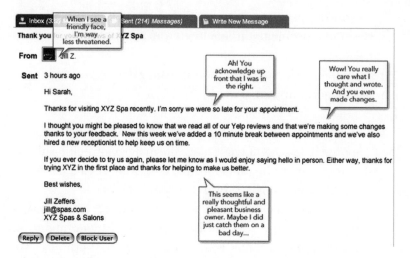

Figure 7.3   What to Do When Responding to Negative Reviews

says bad things about our business, and a negative review can feel like a personal attack.

The good news is that by contacting a reviewer and establishing a genuine human relationship, you have a chance to help the situation and maybe even change the customer's perspective for the better. We've heard lots of success stories from business owners who were polite to their reviewers and were accordingly given a second chance.

But please be careful here. If your reviewer perceives that you are being rude, condescending or disingenuous in any way, there's a chance he or she could get angry and make the situation even worse. Remember, this is a volatile customer who could well copy and paste your message all over the Web!

Remember too that customers' reviews are protected by the First Amendment. Threatening to sue them for libel or slander may feel good in the moment, but odds are slim you'll win if the suit goes to court.

So just keep your message simple, and avoid making excuses or being defensive. Thank your customer for the patronage and the feedback. If you can be specific about the customer's experience and any changes you have made as a result of a problem, this could go very far in earning trust.

To Yelp's advice on responding to negative reviews or comments, we add our own:

- *People want to engage with people.* Be conversational in your response to reviews and talk like a normal person. This isn't the time to use multisyllabic words, corporate speak, language sanitized by attorneys, or industry acronyms.

  For example, how would you feel if you received this boilerplate response to a review or post you made about an exasperating problem you experienced at a business? "We are sorry to hear about the inconvenience, and we appreciate your comments. We are happy that you have spoken up so we can make improvements. We will be working hard to ensure that your next visit is more enjoyable." Without any specifics—or a sense of humanity—in the response, such a canned answer is likely to do more to infuriate reviewers than to calm their ire. Seek to be real, use specifics, and avoid "robotspeak."

- *Work to respond promptly.* If possible, try to respond to web site reviews about your business within 24 hours. (Good tracking software and systems will help make this possible.) Speediness sends a sign to customers that you're watching these sites closely and that you care what people are saying about your organization. Make sure to triage any negative reviews, responding to them first.

- *Avoid excuses or trying to spin the situation to make yourself look like a victim.* The idea is to be open, honest, and sincere. If you know you contributed to a problem in some way or if some part of your business is in obvious need of improvement, apologize sincerely, work to diffuse the situation, and describe what you'll change to ensure that the customer doesn't experience the same problem again.

- *Above all, never, ever lose your head.* The moment you go ballistic or start hurling brickbats, you've lost the battle—and increased the odds that your written response will show up again and again on blogs or other sites around the Web. Take at least 30 minutes after reading a negative comment to digest it and think through a proper response before putting fingers to keyboard. Then let your response sit or "grow cold" for another period of time before returning to edit it with a more detached and balanced eye, keeping in mind how you want your organization to be perceived.

"Hands down, when I've seen conflict on our site, it's usually because the business owner is enraged, furious, or personally hurt," Jeremy Stoppelman, the CEO of Yelp, said in an interview with *The New York Times.*

Tami Cabrera, owner of Muddy Paws Cheesecake, was initially crushed when a negative review of her business popped up on Yelp. Taking time to think about the words and how to proceed, she sent a private message to the reviewer. Follow the trail:

> (1 star) "I'm glad they have vegan and gluten-free options for people who want it but I tried a piece of their pumpkin pie cheesecake and I had to spit it out. I can't even explain the awful taste. To be fair it was the only piece I tried. Maybe someday I'll try something else there. Maybe."
>
> "Hi! I wanted to contact you. I'd like to invite you to our bakery to try several other flavors. I'm sorry you didn't like the pumpkin cheesecake you tried. We've never heard that from anyone before and in fact have never had a bad review in 17 years, so I'm sad to see this review on Yelp. I'd really like to make it up to you by offering you free cheesecake and a chance to win you over :) Our passion is creating the best quality product. We also enjoy giving back to the community including many

animal and children's causes. I feel bad that you had this experience and I'd LOVE to (try) to make it up to you! Cheers, Tami Cabrera, Owner, Muddy Paws Cheesecake"

"HI Tammy. Yes I would try some cheesecake for sure. I don't like giving bad reviews but I also did point out that it was the only kind and time I'd tried your cheesecake. I do like to support locally owned places and would love to give you guys another shot."

As of this writing, the reviewer and Tami have not made an in-person connection. She is hopeful that will happen. Regardless, this demonstrates a very positive response to a negative review.

Responding to Positive Reviews

Yelp's advice:

Responding to positive reviews should be easy, right? It sounds easy, but it's also surprisingly easy to get this wrong. When contacting a person who has left a positive review, your purpose should simply be to deliver a "human" thank-you and let them know you care. That's it. No gift certificates. No mailing lists. No event invites. No reactions to the minor complaint in their reviews.

This may seem counterintuitive, but just try to put yourself in the reviewer's shoes and think about whether you would really want anything other than a simple thank-you. While a gift or invitation sounds nice, it can also be misinterpreted as a bribe or payment for review.

Remember, the customer already likes your business—just use this as an opportunity to thank them and introduce yourself.

Earlier we highlighted Pampered Pooch Playground (see Chapter 5). In searching sites, we found this review and public response on Yelp:

10/26/2009 (3 stars; not a glowing review) "I wish I knew LESS about this place. It's bad enough that you people pay so much money for your dogs to have a private room to 'watch tv' but even worse that you can watch it live from a webcam. Weird."

Comment from Keith M. of Pampered Pooch Playground 10/26/2009: "Why would you not want to take your pooch to a place where you can check up on them and make sure the place is well run. ;)"

Despite the fact that this is not a glowing review, Keith opted to respond in a public arena—short, positive, and supportive of his brand.

Responding in Public versus Private

Yelp also suggests keeping your feedback simple and polite if you're convinced you need to respond publicly to reviews or comments about your business. Most people who use review sites appreciate honesty and like to know when businesses are making changes based on their feedback.

If a review is completely false, it's better to try to resolve the issue through a private message first, Yelp suggests. If you feel a public comment is absolutely needed, present your case as simply and politely as possible, *and do not attack or talk down to the reviewer under any circumstances.* It pays to remember that other potential customers will be reading your comment, and you don't want to give them a negative impression of your business.

In short, Yelp suggests using public comments only to:

- Tell the community at large what you've done to address a specific concern raised by a reviewer
- Provide correct information when a review contains something inaccurate or out of date (for example, reference to an experience with a meal that's not on your menu,

incorrect information about return policies, out-of-date price information, etc.)

• Provide your version of a difficult situation when you're unable to resolve a dispute through private messages; remember to be polite and stick to the facts, Yelp says, since your comments are public and can be seen by potential customers

Responding to Customer Suggestions and Ideas

One of the best ways to show customers that you care about their opinions is to give them a voice in suggesting improvements to your existing products and services as well as helping shape the future of your organization. No one knows your products or services better than people who spend time talking about them online, and smart organizations tap into that brainpower.

Sometimes called *crowdsourcing*, this process gives customers a platform for offering up new product or service ideas, suggested changes to business processes, or other ideas that can benefit them but also boost your company's bottom line. Crowdsourcing initiatives also help customers feel more connected to an organization, since their sense of loyalty grows if their ideas are closely considered and some put into use.

Dell Computer was at the forefront of the crowdsourcing movement with creation of its IdeaStorm concept in 2007. The relevant section on its web site encourages customers and others to submit ideas for new products, technology improvements, or process improvements. The user community then votes for its favorite ideas and demotes ideas it doesn't like. Dell considers the highest-rated ideas for product development concepts or changes.

Here is a short list of ideas offered up to IdeaStorm that Dell subsequently implemented:

• *Expanded offerings of the Linux operating system.* Members of the Linux community were vocal in requesting additional

Dell consumer products that offered the Linux operating system, and the idea received strong voting support. "We went back to the community and asked them what flavors of Linux they wanted, and within six weeks we were offering more laptops with the varieties that received the highest votes," Richard Binhammer of Dell says.

- *Reduced "bloatware."* Customers told Ideastorm they wanted less bloatware, or the software that comes preloaded on some desktops and laptops that often included everything but the kitchen sink, on Dell computers.

    "We looked at the issue and found that in some cases things that were preloaded were even creating software conflicts, so it made sense to eliminate some of it, particularly on our higher-end computers where people were paying a premium price," says Binhammer.

- *Improvements to Dell Mini 10 netbooks and Inspiron Z laptops.* The company implemented submitted ideas for more power, more memory, and using a different variety of the Ubuntu operating system on its Dell Mini 10 netbooks, as well as ideas for thinner and lighter Inspiron Z full-size laptops.

Other companies also are using crowdsourcing with success, highlighted by Starbucks' suggestion forum MyStarBucksIdea .com. Ideas offered up and voted on by customers that Starbucks has implemented include the green splash sticks that, when inserted in sipping holes of coffee cups, reduce spills when in transit; the ability for customers to check their Starbucks card balance at counters without printing a receipt; and discounted shipping rates for Starbucks products sent to military personnel.

Customers Helping Other Customers

Other organizations have figured out that they don't have to bear the whole burden of assisting customers or responding to their questions online; often fellow customers are perfectly willing and able to help out.

Creating online forums where customers can get answers or advice from other customers is an increasingly popular and cost-effective way to respond to customer needs online. Customers post a question or problem about specific products or services, and others jump in to provide advice on how they addressed the issue or provide links to other resources that can help.

SAP, the business software company, created a Communities of Innovation section on its web site, designed to facilitate idea swapping and creative thinking among SAP business process managers and developers; the tool now has more than 1 million users. The idea is to have "customers co-innovate and partners collaborate to achieve results that test cost, time and expertise limitations in everyday business," SAP says. Client companies of SAP are encouraged to use these online communities to gain access to peers and subject matter experts to discuss questions or concerns about SAP products.

How well you respond to customer questions, reviews, problems, and suggestions—and whether you get that response right the first time—separates the customer service champs from the pretenders. Effective response only happens by placing people with strong service aptitudes in contact roles, training them to be as proficient in providing assistance with the written word as the spoken one, and compensating or rewarding them fairly so that they offer continuity of care.

As we've shown time and again, one ill-considered response in today's highly connected world can take years for you to live down.

Chapter 8

PAY ATTENTION TO RECOVERY

One service scenario more than any other gives companies an opportunity to either cement customer loyalty or turn customers into hard-hearted adversaries. When customers experience problems or service breakdowns, the true nature of an organization's commitment to service quality is peeled back and revealed.

Whether an overcooked restaurant meal, a delivered product that arrives with missing parts, or newly installed software with annoying bugs, how you respond—both to the problem and to the emotional state of the customer—determines whether customers sing your praises or go running to their keyboards to tell the world about your callous or indifferent treatment. The stakes for service "recovery" grow even higher when your biggest or best customers experience hiccups in service quality.

As Dr. Leonard Berry, Texas A&M professor and noted service quality researcher, has said, "The acid test of service quality is how you solve customers' problems."

The Dollar Impact of Service Breakdown

Simply mention the name of a cable or Internet service provider and it can send chills down customers' spines; the service reputation of these organizations, well deserved or not, is something less than stellar. TOA Technologies, based in Beachwood, Ohio, provides service solutions to telecommunications, cable, and satellite providers. Out of curiosity and to generate some hard data about customer perceptions, TOA decided to do a survey.[1] Among the top findings of this research was that customers take service missteps very, very personally. Here are a few numbers from the survey:

- Thirty-seven percent of consumers believe that the standard wait window for installers or technicians is four to eight hours because companies "take advantage of the fact people will most likely wait for the service/delivery because they want/need it."
- Eighty-two percent say they wait in their homes, on average, at least one entire day per year for service or deliveries.
- Nearly one in five consumers (18 percent) had lost wages (taken unpaid time off) to wait for service or delivery in their home in the first six months of 2009.
- Fifty-seven percent say that the company providing the service is at fault if the delivery or service technician is late or doesn't show up. Only 19 percent blame the actual driver or technician.

But the real eye opener in the data came in terms of the dollar impact of this perceived shoddy service:

- Eighteen percent of customers have refused or cancelled a product or service because the service or delivery person was late or didn't show up.
- Twenty-nine percent have left their homes in frustration because the service or delivery person was late.

TOA's research echoes our own data as well as that from other notable studies. In short, a failure to respond quickly and appropriately to problems experienced by customers has negative fallout for customer retention and your bottom line. Conversely, solve problems to customers' satisfaction—quickly and with good cheer—and the result can be as though the customer experienced no headache or hassle at all.

Research conducted by TARP Worldwide, an Arlington, Virginia-based market research firm, found that in almost all industries, a customer who complains and is satisfied by the resolution of his complaint is actually 30 percent more loyal than a non-complaining customer and 50 percent more loyal than a complainer who remains unsatisfied.[2] Good service recovery also has a strong correlation to customer retention, which research shows to be one of the best ways to boost profits. Fred Reichheld, a noted researcher in customer loyalty, studied customer retention over a seven-year period in various industries. His calculations of customer retention started with base profit and considered profits from increased purchases, profits from word-of-mouth referrals, and profits from price premium purchases. His findings show that profits from a single customer are not static but increase over time. In other words, a customer who has been with you for seven years can be up to 377 percent more profitable than a customer you have only recently wooed to your products or services.

The bottom-line calculation is that by focusing on customer retention tactics such as service recovery and increasing customer retention by a mere 5 percent, an organization can boost profits up to 75 percent.[3]

An Implied Covenant

At the core of every customer interaction is an overt or implied contract or promise. When organizations keep that promise— which is, in essence, that if customers experience a problem, they'll conduct good-faith efforts to make it right—everyone profits and comes away from the transaction a little bit better for the effort. But fall short of the promise and the negative impact can be felt by everyone involved. There are direct and indirect economic consequences for buyer and seller, giver and receiver. Most customers who feel cheated or misled by a merchant, online or offline, demand their money back and vow to never do business with that merchant again. Even more important, they warn anyone who will listen to steer clear of that company.

Three rules pave the way to effective service recovery in the Paying Attention approach:

- *Rule One: Strive to do it right the first time.* Whether "it" is fixing the car, shipping the product, or resolving a mix-up over a billing error—your systems, policies, and practices should make you ETDBW in your customer's eyes. It should be your platinum standard.

    Effective recovery processes do little good if they're not also accompanied by systems and processes that regularly examine—and fix—the root cause of any service breakdown.
- *Rule Two: Do it very, very right when things have gone wrong for the customer.* And do the "fixing" without leaving the customer with a bad taste in his mouth or a lingering memory of a nightmare experience. It's vital to make the most of these precious second chances for redemption.
- *Rule Three: Most customers do not give you a third chance . . . they simply walk away.* Once they do, never again will they transfer any of their greenbacks into your hands.

What Is Service Recovery?

Service recovery is a focused effort by a service provider to return aggrieved customers to a state of satisfaction after a service or product breakdown. Service recovery is about keeping customers coming back after disaster strikes or even simply if something annoying happens. In simple terms, recovery is the special effort customers expect you to put forward when things have gone a little—or a lot—wrong for them. It is about fixing both the problem and the person.

Effective service recovery that saves at-risk customers for the organization and becomes a competitive distinguisher is not an accident or a random act of will. It is, rather, a planned, systematic process. An effective service recovery system is more than an elaborate apology and monetary make-good effort designed to mollify upset customers and, if necessary, buy back their business.

The core attributes of an effective service recovery system are a clear problem-resolution process, a complaint and problem capture and analysis subsystem, and a way of feeding information on systematic problems back into the system to help reduce their occurrence. At the same time, effective recovery is a set of skillful, real-time actions taken by carefully selected individuals who are trained in the tact and diplomacy necessary to successfully manage an upset, disappointed, or frightened customer.

Successful recovery is the perfect blend of carefully thought-out processes and procedures and skillful, often spontaneous actions. When done well, it can help right even the most grievous wrongs and save customers who already are one step out the door or one click toward the competition.

Five Axioms of Effective Service Recovery

Five self-evident truths, or axioms, underlie customer-centered, effective service recovery philosophy and/or principles. We explore these axioms here.

Axiom 1: Customers Have Recovery Expectations

Expectations are the building blocks of all customer transactions, the embodiment of all customers' wants and needs. A customer's expectations can be as unique as the body shape and inner functioning of a doctor's patient. But just as in medicine, fundamental similarities can guide our efforts. The basic alikeness of two different human kidneys enables physicians to perform kidney surgery using a reliable set of norms, protocols, and prognoses. There is an apt parallel in service—and service recovery—expectations. We all want personalized treatment, but our individual visions of what that entails can share a lot of similarities.

Paying attention to what the customer says, the tone of voice, and the sense of urgency indicates a lot about where the customer's priorities lie. Asking good open-ended questions to engage the customer sends a message that the skills and competence of the service provider are focused on making the experience better for the frustrated consumer. The same holds true with e-mail, Facebook, Twitter, and other sites. Customers who are calling out for help are easy to identify. Are they typing in all caps? Using a lot of exclamation points? Perhaps a lot of symbols? Maybe their 140-character allotment on Twitter says something as simple as, "Please, can't someone help me?" These are major clues. Also remember that most customers are much more informal and comfortable expressing their displeasure online than they are in person. They feel invisible and empowered by anonymity. They have an open forum to vent, and they definitely do. Your charge is to find them and wow them with exceptional service recovery. Change their displeasure to excitement!

Axiom 2: Successful Recovery Is Psychological as Well as Physical: Fix the Person, Then the Problem

Customers who have a problem with your product or service expect you to solve the problem. Just as important but less easy for customers to articulate is the need to be "fixed" psychologically. Often a customer who has a bad experience with your company or product loses faith in your reliability—your ability to deliver what you promised. The repairperson who goes straight to the copier or laptop, completing the repair task and quietly leaves for the next call, may be practicing good technical work-unit-per-hour management, but it's not good recovery. The customer-contact person who needed to use the broken machine and was under pressure to get it fixed needs to be "Repaired" as well. If nothing more, the service person needs to give their contact person an opportunity to vent his pent-up frustration. It is part of the job.

At the core of psychological recovery is restoring trust: the customer's belief that you can and will keep both the explicit and implicit promises you make. Trust is particularly at risk when the customer feels vulnerable, that is, he perceives that all the power to set things right is in your hands and little or nothing is under his control. This vulnerability is of the biggest concern when the customer lacks one of four things:

- *Information.* The customer doesn't know what is going on or how long it will take to set things right. In today's hurry-up world of instant communication, responsiveness is of critical importance. In fact, being proactive rather than reactive may head off many a problem in its making. Give the customer information before she needs it and she'll thank you. Wait until she doesn't have it and you've got a frustrated and angry customer looking to unleash her wrath to anyone who will listen, read, or type back.
- *Expertise.* The customer can't fix the car or computer or fouled-up order or replace the product on his own. All the "smarts" are on the vendor's side. Despite customer intelligence and access to information, it still creates this dilemma. So, when the customer has to wait to have you fix something, it's annoying. You also know how frustrating it is to be forced to send an e-mail to a vendor because no phone number is

listed on their web site and have to wait eight days to get a response—if you get one at all. It's frustrating and can quickly send you looking for answers elsewhere.

- *Freedom.* There is no option for fixing the problem aside from dealing with your company. The customer perceives you as her only hope. It is a disabling, anxiety-rousing situation. If you have a corner on the market or no one else works with your brand, it creates this situation. Whereas that might look great from the organization's side, it's irritating to the customer, especially if the relationship between customer and provider isn't good to begin with. Think of the sound of screeching tires and you have the idea.

- *Recourse.* The customer perceives that when it comes to this computer, car, or malady, you might fix it, but at what cost? The customer wonders how it will be the next time he has to work with you. Will you charge him more for the repair? Or will being honest work against him? We all know that customers aren't always right. But they are, after all, always the customer.

Perhaps one of the biggest challenges for service providers is the number of times they have to fix the same problem over and over again. When dealing with the 14th customer in one day with the same or similar problem, it's tough to stay focused on the customer's needs and not fall into automaton mode. Using the most important "customer-fixing" skill of listening is what keeps the interaction focused on the customer. Whether it's in person or via e-mail, live chat, Facebook, Twitter, or another medium, let the customer tell her story, blow off steam, and give her point of view. When it is appropriate, making a sincere apology focused on the customer's inconvenience goes a long way toward that needed psychological fix. Such an apology sounds like, "I'm sorry you've had to contact us regarding the missing part, Mrs. Fussbudget." This will keep the focus on the customer and start to "fix" the person so you can move on to fixing the problem.

Great Recovery in Action

In her newspaper column, *Everyday Cheapskate*, Mary Hunt, the founder of DebtProofLiving.com, detailed a service recovery experience that not only shows the value of regularly seeking out customer feedback but gives the impression that's made when you quickly fix problems reported by customers.[4] In Hunt's words:

> There's no more competitive business out there these days than there is among hotels in New York City. The survivors are offering great deals on room rates, but that's not enough. They must have impeccable customer service if they plan to attract paying customers.
>
> Take Morgans Hotel on Madison Avenue as an example. I stayed there during a recent trip to New York. It was one of those quick trips; I arrived very late and checked out five hours later. It was not a remarkable experience but not bad, either. In fact, it is not likely I would have given Morgans another thought, except I received an e-mail message asking me for feedback about my stay by filling out a survey.
>
> I don't know that I ever would have contacted Morgans about the absence of a full-length mirror or mentioned the lamps had switches that were so hard to locate I had to get on my hands and knees to find them. Never before had I suggested to management that the carpet in a hotel room needed some attention from stain-removal experts. It wasn't a horrible situation, but I doubt I would have returned.
>
> Because they asked, however, I responded honestly.
>
> Within a matter of days, I received an e-mail response from Debbie Riga, the hotel's general manager. She

(continued)

(*Continued*)

> responded to the problems I mentioned with an apology and commitment to rectify every item I mentioned. Then she offered a free night's stay the next time I was in the city to show her commitment to customer satisfaction.
>
> A return stay confirmed all Riga promised and more, right down to the full-length mirror, easily accessible light switches and pristine carpet. Here's the best part: I've changed my mind about Morgans New York. I will not hesitate to stay there again. More than that, I've just managed to tell 100,000 friends about it, too.

Axiom 3: Work in a Spirit of Partnership

Our research suggests strongly that customers who participate in the problem-solving effort are more satisfied with the problem resolution. There are, however, limits and provisos to this dictum. When the company clearly causes the problem, asking the customer what he would like to see happen next gives the customer a sense of regaining control. That regained sense of control can be vital to calming customers who feel that the organization treated them unjustly or in some way abused them or who are bordering on a perception that they were victimized or treated unfairly.

When the customer clearly caused the problem, asking him to do something to help facilitate solving the problem is appropriate and increases the probability that the customer will feel satisfied with the solution. The solution, in both situations, becomes *our* solution, not *your* solution. One way that organizations using Twitter deal with this is to quickly ask customers to Internet direct-mail (IDM) them pertinent information so that they address the problem in a quick and timely manner. This also takes the problem offline and enables the customer service rep to handle the issue privately rather than in the public domain, which is always a good idea.

Critical to creating a sense of partnership is the way you invite the customer into the problem-solving process. Using those great open-ended questions is a benefit. Ask something like, "How do you see the outcome from your perspective?" Or, "What is your expectation of a satisfactory outcome?" If there is some way to give the customer an assignment to help move the process ahead, that works wonders. The customer provides information that will be helpful to the outcome you have in mind. Or, the customer goes on a hunting expedition to uncover other complications. When a customer forgets to endorse the back of a recently deposited check, it causes a ripple effect of bounced checks. Asking the customer to go into her online banking account and review all the checks she submitted involves her, and the information will be helpful in problem resolution. Do be careful to make sure you use the information the customer provides to guide you to a mutually acceptable conclusion—one that works for the customer and the organization.

Great Recovery in Action

In his "Talking Business" column for the *New York Times*, writer Joe Nocera related a story about Amazon.com that in all likelihood made him a customer for life. Amazon did nothing wrong in this situation, but it nonetheless took responsibility for ensuring a positive outcome for an aggrieved customer.[5] Wrote Nocera:

> My Christmas story, the one I've been telling and retelling, began on Friday, Dec. 21. It was early in the morning, and I had awoken with the sudden, sinking realization that a

(continued)

(*Continued*)

present I bought for one my sons hadn't yet arrived. It wasn't just any present, either. It was a PlayStation 3, a $500 item at the time, and a gift, I happened to know from my sources, that he was hoping for. The PlayStation had come from Amazon.com. So I went to the site and tracked the package. What I saw made my heart sink: the package not only had been shipped, it had been delivered to my apartment building days earlier and signed for by one of my neighbors. I knocked on my neighbor's door, and asked if she still had the PlayStation. No she said; after signing for it, she had put it downstairs in the hallway.

Now I was nearly distraught. In all likelihood, the reason I hadn't seen the package earlier in the week is because it had been stolen, probably by somebody delivering something else to the building. The one thing I knew for sure was it was gone—for which I could hardly blame Amazon.

Nonetheless, I got on the phone with an Amazon customer service representative and explained what had happened. Would Amazon send me a replacement? In my heart of hearts, I knew I didn't have a leg to stand on. I was pleading for mercy.

But the Amazon customer service guy never blinked. After assuring himself that I had never actually touched or seen the PlayStation, he had a replacement on the way before the day was out. It arrived on Christmas Eve. Amazon didn't even charge me for the shipping. My son was very happy. So, of course, was I.

The $500 favor Amazon did for me this Christmas will surely rebound in additional business down the line. Why would I ever shop anywhere else online?

Axiom 4: Customers React More Strongly to "Fairness" Failures Than to "Honest Mistakes"

When customers believe they have been treated unfairly, their reactions tend to be immediate, emotional, and enduring. In other words, if the customer feels that he has been short-changed or disrespected on purpose, the reaction is heated and long lasting.

There is but one course of action a company can take when the customer feels treated unfairly: extreme apology and atonement. Sure, the customer's perception may indeed be the result of a misunderstanding of something said or done and not intended. That is irrelevant. Once a customer feels unfairly treated, you are dealing with an at-risk customer—a customer who is a prime candidate for overt, hostile retaliation. That's when you, as an organization, are the most at risk, particularly with so many new channels of communication available to the customer to express his displeasure. In contrast, admitting an honest mistake seems to knock the wind right out of people, minimizing their full-out emotional response. It often sounds like, "John, I am really sorry I didn't get back to you as promised yesterday. The information was e-mailed to me early this afternoon; I just got sidetracked. It's my error." On hearing a sincere and genuine apology, most of us cut some slack or give grace to the offender. What we really want now is the information.

Perhaps you've been in this same situation: Arriving at the busy restaurant, you are seated. The server acknowledges your presence with a quick greeting and perhaps takes your beverage order. Almost immediately, another party is seated at a table near you. Your server is also assigned that table. Observing the interaction, you see that the other party is treated better (your perception) and their food order is taken first. Now when it comes to your next interaction with the server, what is that like? Brusque? Somewhat irritated? Off-putting? This is what a fairness failure feels like.

For the service provider dealing with a customer who perceives a fairness failure, there is but one course of action: extreme apology and atonement. This at-risk customer wants the organization to put things right and be attentive to his needs.

Axiom 5: Effective Recovery Is a Planned Process

Airlines and hotels overbook. Trains and planes have weather delays and cancellations. If uncontrollable conditions can cause problems for your customers, creating a planned process makes eminent sense. However, you must institute and apply the planned process in a highly responsive, customer–sensitive fashion. Customers remember uncaring or robotic recovery long after they forget the incident that necessitated the solution.

It's of the utmost importance that front-line service employees know what you expect planned recovery to look like and where the limits to recovery lie. Customers remember two things from well-designed and well-implemented planned recovery: the quality of the solutions offered and the skill of the people offering it. Of the two, the latter is the most memorable. Your goal is to create those positive, memorable experiences to keep customers loyal.

Great Recovery in Action

JetBlue Airways has created its own recovery instrument called the Customer Bill of Rights. Published on its web site, this planned recovery process describes how JetBlue will respond if and when things go wrong.

JetBlue Airways' Customer Bill of Rights[6]

Above all else, JetBlue Airways is dedicated to bringing humanity back to air travel. We strive to make every part of your experience as simple and as pleasant as possible. Unfortunately, there are times when things do not go as planned. If you're inconvenienced as a result, we think it is important that you know exactly what you can expect from us. That's why we created our Customer Bill of Rights. These Rights will always be subject to the highest level of safety and security for our customers and crewmembers.

Information

JetBlue will notify customers of the following:
- Delays prior to scheduled departure
- Cancellations and their cause
- Diversions and their cause

Overbookings

Customers who are involuntarily denied boarding shall receive $1,000.

DELAYS (Departure Delays or Onboard Ground Delays on Departure)

For customers whose flight is delayed 3 hours or more after scheduled departure, JetBlue will provide free movies on flights that are 2 hours or longer.

Onboard Ground Delays

JetBlue will provide customers experiencing an Onboard Ground Delay with 36 channels of DIRECTV®*, food and drink, access to clean restrooms and, as necessary, medical treatment. For customers who experience an Onboard Ground Delay for more than 5 hours, JetBlue will also take necessary action so that customers may deplane.

(*continued*)

(*Continued*)

Arrivals:

1. Customers who experience an Onboard Ground Delay on Arrival for 1–1:59 hours after scheduled arrival time are entitled to a $50 Voucher good for future travel on JetBlue.
2. Customers who experience an Onboard Ground Delay on Arrival for 2 hours or more after scheduled arrival time are entitled to a Voucher good for future travel on JetBlue in the amount paid by the customer for the round trip (or the one-way trip, doubled).

Departures:

1. Customers who experience an Onboard Ground Delay on Departure after scheduled departure time for 3–3:59 hours are entitled to a $50 Voucher good for future travel on JetBlue.
2. Customers who experience an Onboard Ground Delay on Departure after scheduled departure time for 4–4:59 hours are entitled to a Voucher good for future travel on JetBlue in the amount paid by the customer for the one-way trip (or $50, whichever is greater).
3. Customers who experience an Onboard Ground Delay on Departure for 5 hours or more after scheduled arrival time are entitled to a Voucher good for future travel on JetBlue in the amount paid by the customer for the round trip (or the one-way trip, doubled).

In-flight entertainment:

JetBlue offers 36 channels of DIRECTV® service on its flights in the Continental U.S. If our LiveTV™ system is inoperable on flights in the Continental U.S., customers are entitled to a $15 Voucher good for future travel on JetBlue.

Cancellations

All customers whose flight is cancelled by JetBlue will, at the customer's option, receive a full refund or reaccommodation on the next available JetBlue flight at no additional charge or fare. If JetBlue cancels a flight within 4 hours of scheduled departure and the cancellation is due to a Controllable Irregularity, JetBlue will also issue the customer a $50 Voucher good for future travel on JetBlue.

Departure Delays

1. Customers whose flight is delayed for 1–1:59 hours after scheduled departure time due to a *Controllable Irregularity* are entitled to a $25 Voucher good for future travel on JetBlue.

2. Customers whose flight is delayed for 2–4:59 hours after scheduled departure time due to a *Controllable Irregularity* are entitled to a $50 Voucher good for future travel on JetBlue.

3. Customers whose flight is delayed for 5–5:59 hours after scheduled departure time due to a *Controllable Irregularity* are entitled to a Voucher good for future travel on JetBlue in the amount paid by the customer for the one-way trip (or $50, whichever is greater).

4. Customers whose flight is delayed for 6 or more hours after scheduled departure time due to a *Controllable Irregularity* are entitled to a Voucher good for future travel on JetBlue in the amount paid by the customer for the round trip (or the one-way trip, doubled).

Seeing Complaints as a Gift

It's always interesting when we ask clients the question, Do you like to deal with frustrated and complaining customers? It's rare that anyone responds with "Absolutely, that's my favorite part of my job." After all, few of us like to deal with people who are unhappy or who are perhaps even saying unsavory things about our mothers.

But a shift in perspective can help associates view complaints differently. When a customer takes the time to complain or offer a suggestion or an idea for improvement, organizations should see those comments as gifts. Yes, gifts. A customer who could have simply walked away because of a problem or out of dissatisfaction is taking time to tell you about the situation—and most important, giving you an opportunity to fix it. That's a real gift.

eBags.com, the massive online e-tailer for all things baggage— luggage, backpacks, handbags, and more—was recognized as e-tailer of the year in 2009 by *Accessories* magazine. Now in business for 10 years, eBags has shipped over 10.21 million bags, and it takes customer complaints seriously—one might say as gifts. Peter Cobb, eBags.com cofounder, relates the story of one customer who purchased a laptop case. After posting a negative review of the case on the eBags.com site, the customer took pictures of the bag and included suggestions on how to improve it in an e-mail to the eBags.com staff. Rather than simply writing off the rant, the staff took it seriously. Working with the manufacturer, improvements were made to the design of the laptop case. It is now one of eBags.com's top-selling items. Cobb can bring to mind 10 examples of similar situations that have brought about changes to bags. This is the perfect demonstration of seeing complaints as gifts and using customer feedback to continuously improve your operations.[7]

Fix the Process to Reduce Recovery Needs

Even when your processes are working well, there's always room for improvement. At Pleasanton, California-based NuCompass Mobility, an independent relocation company, customers complained about the claims process after their furniture was shipped. Despite their service ratings far exceeding industry standards, the service team at NuCompass wanted to make some changes based on customer feedback. The results have been impressive. Here employees saw an opportunity to make improvements when most organizations would have lived with the status quo. Seeking out customer feedback, and taking it seriously, is what differentiates the real service leaders from the wannabes. Here Kathy Cohn, vice president of business process, shares some details on NuCompass Mobility's Customer Process Improvement Initiative.

Great Recovery in Action

When an employee transfers from one location to another, companies often provide relocation assistance, including moving their household goods. Moving someone's personal possessions and furniture presents many opportunities for damage. It is estimated that between 20–25 percent of all shipments include a claim for damage or loss.

As part of the overall relocation process, NuCompass Mobility Services Inc. has focused on household goods shipments for several years, recognizing that it is a tipping point for a successful relocation. Its staff worked with moving companies to institute a more consistent, high-quality customer service process across all moves. As a result, customers' shipment claims have been reduced to an average of 8–10 percent, well below industry norms.

NuCompass Mobility reviews survey data weekly, monthly, and quarterly to spot problem areas for immediate attention and longer-term trends. During the quarterly reviews, the company noticed that even though claims were very low, those same customers were unclear about the claims process

(continued)

(*Continued*)

and status. To improve reliability, NuCompass developed a program to standardize communication by employees and suppliers so that all customers were advised of the process with consistent language and frequency.

The Goal. Improve customer understanding of the claims process and instill confidence that the claim would be resolved quickly. To do this, NuCompass Mobility interviewed customers to better understand their expectations and analyzed the claims process with that information in mind.

The group increased communication touchpoints with customers and moving company representatives and incorporated a review of the survey comments into the monthly moving company meetings. NuCompass set requirements for the timeliness of each communication and linked it to a part of the claims process: the delivery and notice of damage, receipt of a claim form, adjustor's report, and settlement of the claim, as well as biweekly reviews of any outstanding claims. Furthermore, a claims process reminder was added to the forms. Before launching the new process, NuCompass trained its employees and the moving companies' employees on their customers' expectations and the new process.

The Result. NuCompass Mobility monitored customers' reaction to the changes using detailed surveys. After one year, its customer survey data revealed an 118 percent improvement in the top rank (those who strongly agree) related to moving services.

Service Recovery Process

In our more than two decades of research into recovery behaviors and attitudes that customers expect and find memorable, we

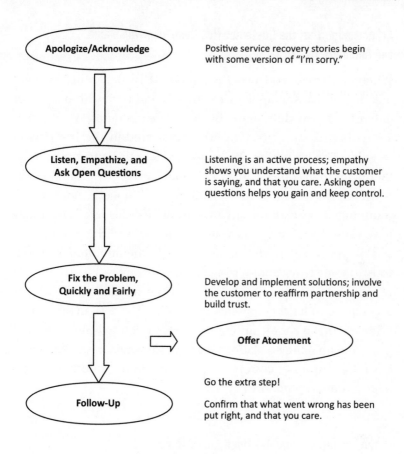

Figure 8.1 The Service Recovery Process

developed a process for handling the spectrum of unhappy customers, from the mildly disappointed to the toxically ticked-off (see Figure 8.1).[8] Applied consistently by customer contact people, the Service Recovery Process has led to an average 12-point improvement in customer ratings of organizations' problem-solving abilities.

Acknowledge That the Customer Has Been Inconvenienced and Apologize for It

Whether it's in person, over the phone, via Twitter, or in an e-mail, it is critical that you apologize without condition, with no hint of defensiveness or shifting the blame to the customer. We find that an apology is most powerful when delivered in the first-person singular. The corporate "We're sorry" lacks the sincerity and authenticity that comes with a personal, verbal acknowledgment delivered on behalf of the organization. A sincere, nonrobotic-sounding "I'm sorry for any inconvenience this late arrival may have caused you" suggests that the pilot or lead flight attendant is taking personal, professional interest in the situation. And contrary to some fears, apologizing for the customer's inconvenience is not, and cannot be, interpreted as an admission of guilt or acceptance of legal culpability or liability. There is, in fact, some evidence that a simple apology alone can defuse a situation and prevent damaging escalation. We have shown time and again the harm that an upset customer with access to the Internet can do to corporate reputations.

Listen, Empathize, and Ask Open-Ended Questions

There is a clear and important difference between empathy and sympathy. Customers do not want service professionals to join them in "Those guys in shipping should be shot" tirades. Rather, customers are looking for a good listener who allows them to explain their point of view and vent their frustrations, who shows an understanding of their upset, and who, by hearing them out, offers tacit evidence of believing the customer's report of the incident or error.

Offer a Fair Fix to the Problem

After the service provider acknowledges and addresses the emotional side of the service breakdown, he must correct the customer's problem. It is important that the customer perceives the service provider as knowledgeable, empowered, and focused on a timely resolution. Contrary to common belief, customers typically bring a sense of fair play to the table when a situation calls for recompense or compensation. If the service provider offers a rational explanation and demonstrated sensitivity and concern, the customer usually responds in kind.

Providing a full explanation of what happened and what will happen to fix the problem is critical. TARP Worldwide has found employees' inability to explain reasons for a breakdown to be the most prevalent cause of customer frustration in recovery efforts and the most easily fixed through training.

In most instances of recovery, these first three actions suffice to fix your customer's problem and patch up the relationship. Approximately 70 percent of service recovery incidents require no gesture of atonement and only a minimal amount of follow-up.

Offer Some Value-Added Atonement for the Inconvenience or Injury

We also call this *symbolic atonement*. Symbolic atonement is the free-dessert, 2 percent discount on your monthly statement, or partial or full refund offer that compensates the customer for inconvenience or distress.

At the most basic level, atonement is a gesture that clearly says, "We want to apologize to you for your inconvenience." Atonement is more than simply the "It's on us," "Free drink," "No charge" offer. It is a demonstration of goodwill. The word *symbolic* is carefully chosen. It suggests that little things, when sincerely done, mean a lot to the customer. Most customers don't expect us to offer to terminate an employee or provide a free trip to Disney World for keeping them waiting in the reception area an extra 10 minutes. They *do* expect a reasonable, small gesture that acknowledges the inconvenience.

Sometimes, however, a custom-tailored or highly aggressive act of atonement might be necessary to keep a highly valued or long-time customer. Furthermore, sometimes a determined, proactive effort can both impress the customer and give your organization's reputation a nice boost. Because today's customer can get a rapid response via Facebook, Twitter, or live chat, it can be that much easier to personalize and tailor the atonement to the customer quickly and effectively.

Keep Your Promises

Customers often are skeptical of a company's recovery promises. Their tendency is to believe that service representatives' promises aim primarily at getting the customer off the phone or away from the service desk rather than actually solving the problem or fixing the customer's upset. Although bad news can prompt the customer to huff and bluster at the customer-contact employee or create a negative review, customers would rather hear straight talk or bad news than be told lies or misleading information. Customers value and happily share with others the feats of customer service representatives who display a "can do" attitude and ability. Here's a great example from Yelp.com:

> "So after I knocked down Pampered Pooch after a not so pleasant experience with one of the employees, the owner Keith immediately reached out to me to get the details of the situation so it could be corrected. He was genuinely concerned about Lucy (our beagle) and us not having a 5 star service experience at his business. Once the details were received about the time/day we were there, he reviewed the tapes and let us know the situation would be handled asap and gave us a free day of daycare (not necessary but much appreciated). Will go back and is now highly recommended based on the genuine concern we received . . . Lucy our beagle couldn't be happier :)" 3/23/2009

Follow-Up

Customers also are favorably impressed when a sales or service person follows up with them after the initial service recovery episode to make sure the solution is still satisfactory. With the myriad communication options available today, such follow-up is easier than ever. Following up gives the organization a second chance to solve the customer's problem if the first effort falls short of the customer's expectations, especially if the customer was reluctant to voice the complaint to you a second time.

Follow-up also is important internally, within the organization. Associates should be able to communicate easily inside their organizations to ensure that the solutions they put in motion actually are executed and to allow recurring problems to be tracked, studied, and removed from the delivery system. Without internal follow-up, service recovery is a one-shot, spray-and-pray activity, not part of a planned, systematic effort to track and reduce service-related problems. In most cases, it is wise to follow up inside your organization prior to contact with the customer so that it's easy to confirm that the billing error, reinstatement of the account, or new shipment has happened.

Key Service Recovery Skills

With a good service recovery process in place, it's up to your staff to execute it. We've identified several key service skills needed to make recovery efforts even more memorable for customers:

- *Empathy.* Make a personal connection.
- *Questioning.* Ask good questions to get at the heart of the problem.
- *Listening.* Demonstrate that you understand the problem from the customer's point of view.
- *Responsiveness.* Find a quick and satisfactory solution.

In today's world of instant communication, customers often expect they'll get a response to their problems immediately. How you define "immediately" will vary by communication medium.

But you can bet that it's definitely to your advantage to respond sooner rather than later. Many companies use tracking software to monitor mention of their companies or brands in online communities; that way, no sooner is a negative comment made than a company representative will respond.

Responsiveness in other mediums will vary. Our experience with thousands of seminar participants indicates that most customers generally expect response to a message left on company voice mail within one hour. In addition, according to data from the U.S. Scorecard Survey (Convergys, 2008), if a customer with a problem or concern does call and speak to a human being, the customer wants her concern cleared up with that one contact. If she has to call back, satisfaction drops considerably.

When it comes to e-mail response, most customers expect an almost immediate acknowledgment of an inquiry, then a more personal and detailed response within a standard eight-hour business day, at a minimum. Many service-focused companies use a four-hour response standard or even two hours when customers have experienced problems or snafus.

Great Recovery in Action

Edward Albro, who works for *PC World* magazine, had a service recovery experience with Netflix, the DVD rental company that impressed him so much he felt compelled to retell it for his magazine's readers. His experience illustrates the powerful word of mouth (factoring in all the magazine's readers) that can result from companies handling problems or complaints effectively.[9] In Albro's words:

> Last night my wife mentioned that she had a hard time streaming a movie included in Netflix's Instant Watching service to our PC. I didn't think too much of it at the time.

After all, the problem could have been with our Internet service provider, our wireless network or our PC. It's the kind of problem that can have so many different fathers that establishing paternity later seldom seems worth the effort.

But this morning, I got an e-mail from Netflix. It said their records indicated we might have had a streaming problem, apologized for the glitch, and offered me a 2 percent discount on my next bill. Here's how the e-mail read:

Dear Ed,

Last night, you may have had trouble watching movies or TV shows instantly on your computer due to technical issues on the website.

We are sorry for the inconvenience this may have caused. If you were unable to watch a movie or TV show last night due to the technical issues on the website, please click the link below and we'll apply a 2 percent credit to your next billing statement.

Again, we apologize for any inconvenience, and thank you for understanding. If you need further assistance, please call us at 1-866-923-0898.

—The Netflix Team

What hoops did I have to jump through to get my discount? Call Netflix and wait on hold for 10 minutes? Fill out an online form documenting exactly what happened and when? Nope. All I had to do was click a link in the e-mail. I was taken to Netflix's site, where I saw a message that my discount would be applied to my next bill.

Technology companies take note. *This is how you provide great customer service.* We consumers all know that things can go wrong with any technology device or service. When

(*continued*)

(*Continued*)

things do blow up, companies should take responsibility and offer amends, making the process as simple as possible for consumers. That's the kind of behavior that breeds customer loyalty.

A lot of customer service execs I've met would probably say that that kind of customer service costs too much. But Netflix has been known for customer service like this since its inception and somehow this former startup has managed to grow and prosper while their behemoth competition, Blockbuster, is tied up in such serious debt problems it is closing retail stores.

Seems like treating your customers well may pay off.

Internal customers should be granted the same or faster response time than external customers. After all, they are supporting the external customer in some way, too. In addition to the quick response time expected by customers, it is always a good plan to be proactive. Alerting the customer of a change in shipping, short shipment, back order, or out of stock situations garners many kudos. Better to be ahead of the issue than to react to it when the customer is frustrated, angry, or out of sorts. When a customer is responding to a problem situation or filing a complaint, it's best to address the concern immediately. Return phone calls, answer e-mails promptly, and move the priority to the top of the list.

Making a personal connection with a customer in a recovery situation is critically important. Using an empathy statement to let him know you are tuned in helps neutralize the emotion. A simple "I can hear your frustration about the partial shipment" can connect at a very personal level. Acknowledging the emotion and restating the situation as you understand it shows your customer you value him. It sends the message that you are ready to help and attend to his needs. Whether it is via e-mail, phone,

Facebook, or in person, a simple, sincere empathy statement goes a long way to winning over the customer.

Great Recovery in Action
Service Recovery Memory Makers

In research that we conducted on what makes for a positive recovery experience, customers in over 90 focus groups told us the elements of recovery that matter most to them. We know that recovery is about fixing the problem and fixing the person. As you look at the list, Figure 8.2, ask yourself which of these speak to fixing the problem. The answer is – none of them. Each of these Memory Makers addresses fixing the person. That's why we say – Fix the person first, then solve the problem – to create those positive, memorable experiences.

1. Dealt with upset	79.0%
2. Apologized	69.1%
3. Showed humility/poise	62.9%
4. Followed up afterwards	56.8%
5. Showed problem-solving skill	53.0%
6. Admitted organizational error, when appropriate	44.4%
7. Acted fully empowered	40.7%
8. Showed good listening	40.7%
9. Showed empathy	38.3%
10. Acted with urgency	35.8%
11. Created value added	32.1%
12. Believed the customer	24.7%

Figure 8.2   Service Recovery Memory Makers

Once a connection is made with a strong empathy statement and the customer is assured you are with them, you are likely to need more information. Asking those valuable open-ended questions will encourage participation and get you the highest-quality information. These questions typically start with the basic "w's": who, what, where, and when. In addition, the indirect openers such as "Give me an example of . . .," "Describe for me . . .," or "Tell me about . . ." require an answer beyond the simple "yes" or "no" responses to closed-ended questions.

It's our rule of thumb that the more emotional the customer, the more important it is to use open-ended questions. A good way to be sure that you have these questions at hand is to brainstorm a list of typical problems or complaints you receive, then generate a list of questions to ask a customer who might bring up such problems or complaints. If you find you are challenged getting a customer to work with you, it's very likely that only closed-ended questions are being asked. Switch to open-ended questions and the tone of the conversation will change. Note that in the list of the basic "w's" for open-ended questions, the "why" is omitted. Asking a "why-based" question puts the customer on the defensive. When a customer is already frustrated, angry, or confused, the last thing you want is to make her defensive. Avoid the "why-based" questions at all costs.

When it's time for the customer to respond, it's also time for you to quiet your mind and listen. And, as much as we think we all listen quite well, it's another thing to demonstrate that overtly to the customer. Using effective listening techniques such as summarizing, paraphrasing, or repeating only gets you part of the way up the Pay Attention ladder. Demonstrating how much you value the customer takes you to the next level. Simple statements such as "I'm glad you suggested that" or "I really like that idea" send the message that you value the customer's input. Or you might ask the customer his opinion or advice, to show your interest and appreciation for his time.

Particularly in emotionally fraught recovery situations, service providers get caught in those pesky "mental detours"—thinking of their next question, formulating a response to the customer's question, or wondering what's for lunch today. Each time we take the detour, we miss valuable information or cues from our customers. Practice taking notes, using active listening techniques, or simply suspending judgment until you have thoroughly listened to your customer. You have plenty of time to respond in the most appropriate way.

Effective service recovery that saves customers at risk of defection—or of badmouthing your company to all who will listen—is not simply the spontaneous act of good-hearted employees. It is, instead, a planned and systematic process that relies on actions taken by carefully selected employees trained in the art of soothing confused, upset, or disappointed customers. When executed well, service recovery is far more than a loss leader; it is an essential tool for enhancing customer retention and adding profit to your bottom line.

Notes

Chapter 2 Pay Attention to Your Marketing Message

1. As reported on Fox News Channel News, August 22, 2009.

Chapter 3 Pay Attention to Preparation

1. "Hire for Attitude, Train for Skill," Peter Carbonara, *Fast Company*, December 18, 2007.
2. "Implications of Corporate Culture: A Manager's Guide to Action," in *Organizational Dynamics,* Autumn 1983, p. 8.
3. "The 2009 List of Customer Service Champs," Jena McGregor, Aili McConnon, and David Kiley, *BusinessWeek*, February 19, 2009.
4. Ibid.
5. "Social Networking: A Force for Development," Marjorie Derven, *Training and Development Journal,* July 2009.
6. "The 2008 List of Customer Service Champs," Jena McGregor, *Business-Week*, February 21, 2008.
7. "Ultimate Software Puts Employees First," Workforce Management Online, July 2, 2009.

Chapter 4 Pay Attention to the Customer Experience

1. "The 2009 List of Customer Service Champs," Jena McGregor, Aili McConnon, and David Kiley, *BusinessWeek*, February 19, 2009.

2. "Comcast's Twitter Man," Rebecca Reisner, *BusinessWeek*, January 13, 2009.
3. "Can Comcast Make a Connection?" Suzanne Ziegler, *Minneapolis Star Tribune*, August 25, 2009.
4. "The sales picture brightens after a redesign at The Artful Home," InternetRetailer.com, February 5, 2008.

Chapter 5 Pay Attention to New Feedback Channels

1. The concept of the Net Promoter is defined in the book *The Ultimate Question*, by Fred Reichheld, Harvard Business Press, 2006.
2. *E-Service: 24 Ways to Keep Your Customers When the Competition Is Just a Click Away*, Ron Zemke and Tom Connellan, AMACOM Books, 2000.

Chapter 6 Pay Attention to Your Reaction

1. "Target Tells Blogger to Go Away," Michael Barbaro, *New York Times*, January 28, 2008.
2. "Whole Foods Devotees Lash Out at CEO; Customers, Angry Over His Health-Care Views, Share Feelings of Betrayal on Web," Ylan Q Mui, *Washington Post,* August 19, 2009.
3. "Good Reasons to Post Customer Reviews on Your Site," Douglas Gantenbein, Microsoft.com's *Midsize Business*.

Chapter 8 Pay Attention to Recovery

1. TOA Technologies, Press release, Survey listed on their web site, published in September 2009; www.toatech.com, p. 1.
2. *Strategic Customer Service: Managing the Customer Experience to Increase Positive Word of Mouth, Build Loyalty, and Maximize Profits*, John A. Goodman, AMACOM Books, 2009, p. 19.
3. *The Ultimate Question*, Fred Reichheld, Harvard Business Press, 2006, p. 2.
4. *Everyday Cheapskate: Make Great Customer Service Work for You*, Mary Hunt, St. Paul Pioneer Press, September 21, 2009.
5. "Put Buyers First: What a Concept," Joe Nocera, *New York Times*, January 5, 2008
6. JetBlue Airways' Customer Bill of Rights, www.jetblue.com/about/ourcompany/promise/index.html, p. 10.
7. "It's in the Bag," Lauren Parker, *Accessories,* October 2009.
8. *Knock Your Socks Off Service Recovery*, Ron Zemke and Chip R. Bell, AMACOM Books, New York, 1997, p. 14.
9. "NetFlix: Now This Is Customer Service," Edward Albro, *PC World*, May 15, 2009.

About the Authors

Ann Thomas brings more than 20 years of experience in consulting and training to each of her clients. Her work has been focused in the areas of improving service quality, diversity awareness, generational differences, sales, performance management, and professional development.

A senior consultant and lead facilitator with Performance Research Associates since 1999, Ann's clients include Atlanta Hartsfield-Jackson International Airport; Depository Trust and Clearing Corporation; Marriott ExecuStay; The Mall of America; NuCompass Mobility Services; Turner Broadcasting; Advantage Health Systems; Accenture; The Securities Exchange Commission; Daimler Chrysler; Plexent; Universities of Connecticut, Alabama, Iowa, Kansas, and Texas; Inter-American Development Bank; National Geospacial Agency; The Chicago Mercantile Exchange; and many others.

Ann does extensive volunteer work within her community. In her off hours Ann enjoys working in her garden, walking, sailing, and spending time with her family.

Jill Applegate is the project manager and client coordinator with Performance Research Associates. She served as right hand to the late Ron Zemke for nearly 15 years and takes seriously the responsibility of wowing customers on a daily basis.

Jill works closely with clients to ensure that our collaborative efforts hit the mark. Her responsiveness, attention to detail, and depth of knowledge allow her to not only talk the talk, but also walk the walk.

Jill stays busy volunteering in her church, playing the piano, watching football, and taking frequent trips to Walt Disney World and other theme parks, and is proud of her up-to-date roller coaster resume.

Index